The Israeli Secret Services

INTERNATIONAL ORGANIZATIONS SERIES

General Editors:
Robert G. Neville (Executive Editor)
John J. Horton

Robert A. Myers John Paxton
Ian Wallace Hans H. Wellisch

John J. Horton is Deputy Librarian of the University of Bradford and currently Chairman of its Academic Board of Studies in Social Sciences. He has maintained a longstanding interest in the discipline of area studies and its associated bibliographical problems, with special reference to European Studies. In particular he has published in the field of Icelandic and of Yugoslav studies, including the two relevant volumes in the World Bibliographical Series.

Robert A. Myers is Associate Professor of Anthropology in the Division of Social Sciences and Director of Study Abroad Programs at Alfred University, Alfred, New York. He has studied post-colonial island nations of the Caribbean and has spent two years in Nigeria on a Fulbright Lectureship. His interests include international public health, historical anthropology and developing societies. In addition to Amerindians of the Lesser Antilles: a bibliography (1981), A Resource Guide to Dominica, 1493-1986 (1987) and numerous articles, he has compiled the World Bibliographical Series volumes on Dominica (1987), Nigeria (1989) and Ghana (1991).

John Paxton was the editor of The Statesman's Year-Book from 1969 to 1990. His published works include The Developing Common Market, The Dictionary of the European Communities (which was commended by the McColvin Medal Committee of the British Library Association), The Penguin Dictionary of Abbreviations, The Penguin Dictionary of Proper Names (with G. Paton), Companion to Russian History, Companion to the French Revolution, and The Statesman's Year-Book Gazetteer. He was also chief consultant editor of the New Illustrated Everyman's Encyclopaedia.

Ian Wallace is Professor of German at the University of Bath. A graduate of Oxford in French and German, he also studied in Tübingen, Heidelberg and Lausanne before taking teaching posts at universities in the USA, Scotland and England. He specializes in contemporary German affairs, especially literature and culture, on which he has published numerous articles and books. In 1979 he founded the journal GDR Monitor, which he continues to edit under its new title German Monitor.

Hans H. Wellisch is Professor emeritus at the College of Library and Information Services, University of Maryland. He was President of the American Society of Indexers and was a member of the International Federation for Documentation. He is the author of numerous articles and several books on indexing and abstracting, and has published The Conversion of Scripts and Indexing and Abstracting: an International Bibliography, and Indexing from A to Z. He also contributes frequently to Journal of the American Society for Information Science, The Indexer and other professional journals.

VOLUME 13

The Israeli Secret Services

Frank A. Clements
Compiler

Transaction Publishers
NEW BRUNSWICK (U.S.A.) AND LONDON (U.K.)

Second paperback printing 2009
First paperback printing © 2008 by Transaction Publishers, New Brunswick, New Jersey. Originally published in 1996 by ABC-CLIO Ltd.

All rights reserved under International and Pan-American Copyright Conventions. No part of this book may be reproduced or transmitted in any form or by any means, electronic or mechanical, including photocopy, recording, or any information storage and retrieval system, without prior permission in writing from the publisher. All inquiries should be addressed to Transaction Publishers, Rutgers—The State University, 35 Berrue Circle, Piscataway, New Jersey 08854-8042.

This book is printed on acid-free paper that meets the American National Standard for Permanence of Paper for Printed Library Materials.

Library of Congress Catalog Number: 96-17331
ISBN: 978-1-56000-228-4 (cloth) ; 978-1-4128-0814-9 (paper)
Printed in the United States of America

              Library of Congress Cataloging-in-Publication Data

Clements, Frank, 1942-
    Israeli Secret Services / Frank A. Clements.
      p. cm.—(International organizations series : v. 13)
    Includes bibliographical references and index.
    ISBN 1-56000-228-X (alk. paper)
      1. Israel. Mosad le-modi' in ve-tafkidim meyuhadim—Bibliography.
  2. Intelligence service—Israel—Bibliography. 3. Secret service—Israel—Bibliography. I. Title. II. Series: International organizations series (New Brunswick, N. J.) : v. 13.

Z6724.I7C54   1996
[JQ 1830.A56I6]
016.327125694—dc20   96-17331

INTERNATIONAL ORGANIZATIONS SERIES

Each volume in the International Organizations Series is either devoted to one specific organization, or to a number of different organizations operating in a particular region, or engaged in a specific field of activity. The scope of the series is wide-ranging and includes intergovernmental organizations, international non-governmental organizations, and national bodies dealing with international issues. The series is aimed mainly at the English-speaker and each volume provides a selective, annotated, critical bibliography of the organization, or organizations, concerned. The bibliographies cover books, articles, pamphlets, directories, databases and theses and, wherever possible, attention is focused on material about the organizations rather than on the organizations' own publications. Notwithstanding this, the most important official publications, and guides to those publications, will be included. The views expressed in individual volumes, however, are not necessarily those of the publishers.

VOLUMES IN THE SERIES

1 *European Communities*, John Paxton
2 *Arab Regional Organizations*, Frank A. Clements
3 *Comecon: The Rise and Fall of an International Socialist Organization*, Jenny Brine
4 *International Monetary Fund*, Anne C. M. Salda
5 *The Commonwealth*, Patricia M. Larby and Harry Hannam
6 *The French Secret Services*, Martyn Cornick and Peter Morris
7 *Organization of African Unity*, Gordon Harris
8 *North Atlantic Treaty Organization*, Phil Williams
9 *World Bank*, Anne C. M. Salda
10 *United Nations System*, Joseph Preston Baratta
11 *The Organization of American States*, David Sheinin
12 *British Secret Services*, Philip H. J. Davies
13 *Israeli Secret Services*, Frank A. Clements

Contents

INTRODUCTION	ix
INTELLIGENCE SERVICES: GENERAL WORKS	1
ISRAELI INTELLIGENCE: GENERAL	7
MOSSAD: GENERAL	13
MILITARY INTELLIGENCE	25
PALESTINE: ILLEGAL IMMIGRATION	27
ANTI-NAZI OPERATIONS	32
ARAB–ISRAELI WARS	34
PALESTINE LIBERATION ORGANIZATION	39
FOREIGN INCURSIONS	46
General 46	
Operations against Iraq 48	
Lebanese incursions 50	
Relations with the United States and US Intelligence 52	
RESCUE OPERATIONS	58
INDEX OF AUTHORS	61
INDEX OF TITLES	65
INDEX OF SUBJECTS	71

Introduction

The Institute for Intelligence and Special Services, or the Mossad as it is better known, has long had the confidence of the Israeli population, a privilege not shared by other intelligence services in the Western world. This is largely explained by the creation of the State of Israel in 1948, an event which was followed by a period of isolation, military threats on all of its borders, and guerrilla attacks within its borders. The support enjoyed by the Mossad, however, was demonstrated in utter secrecy as, until the 1970s, the existence of the organization was not acknowledged within Israel.

In order to understand the present-day situation and the development and effectiveness of the Mossad, it is necessary to go back to the period before the creation of the State of Israel, for this branch of Israeli intelligence has its roots in the pre-Second World War situation in Palestine and Europe.

The Jewish struggle against the British administration and the Arabs during the period of the Mandate gave rise to a number of underground organizations both within Palestine and also among the Jewish communities, especially in Europe. As the Jews were a minority population in a strongly contested state, the Jewish Agency for Palestine's priority was the encouragement of Jewish emigration. This was contrary to the terms of the Mandate and the policy of the British authorities.

Illegal immigration from Europe was encouraged but on a relatively small scale until the real impact of the policies of the Third Reich began to be felt in the late 1930s. Germany's policy towards its Jewish population began to cause alarm amongst sections of the population and also gave rise to anti-Semitic feeling in other countries in Europe,

Introduction

especially in Eastern Europe and France. Consequently the Jewish underground discovered that it had a large-scale operation on its hands, both in terms of numbers and also on account of the logistical problems of dealing with regimes that were becoming more hostile and less likely to acquiesce in the process. It was from this ferment that the Mossad Aliyah Beth developed, in order to provide the clandestine network of agents and the infrastructure necessary to secure emigration from Europe to Palestine. It gradually built up a network of Jewish agents and sympathizers throughout Europe and was funded by the Jewish Agency for Palestine and the wider Jewish community. Countries such as Yugoslavia were used as staging posts, with ships being chartered to land immigrants on the Palestine coast, usually at night, at which time another network took over to evade the British authorities. Operations were carried out against a backcloth of strictly controlled legal immigration and a British policy of deportation of illegal immigrants, designed to satisfy the terms of the Mandate and also to suppress opposition from the majority Arab population.

The appearance of concentration camps in Germany accelerated the emigration from Europe as it became a question of survival for the Jewish population. Accordingly, the operations of the Jewish underground became more sophisticated, organized and dangerous. The costs of the operation also increased as the price of documents, bribes and shipping rose in line with the risk factor.

The conclusion of the war in Europe brought no relief to the operation, since by then the number of displaced persons in Europe ran into millions and the world at large became aware of the horrors of the Holocaust. However, restrictions on legal immigration into Palestine were still being enforced by the British Mandatory administration in line with the perceived terms and spirit of the Mandate. The Jewish underground, therefore, continued to operate and, as a result of the Holocaust, became more militant. The volume of illegal immigration increased and soon the British administration was powerless to control the flow.

Eventually the British government determined that the Palestine Mandate was no longer a responsibility that it could discharge, the policies being pursued satisfied neither the Arab nor Jewish populations in Palestine, or the wider Jewish community, or the Jewish lobby in the United States. The British government therefore handed the problem over to the newly established United Nations. The Jewish underground reacted immediately and effectively seized power, waging war against the surrounding Arab armies whilst the question of recognition of the state was still being considered by the United Nations.

Introduction

The fledgling State of Israel was born out of armed conflict in May 1948 and was surrounded by enemies who had suffered a bitter and ignominious defeat. Also, in spite of their defeat, the combined forces of the Arab states were still superior in terms of numbers and equipment. In addition, the majority of the population were Arabs in spite of the thousands that had fled as refugees in May 1948 and were therefore antagonistic towards the new state. It was recognized from the outset by David Ben-Gurion and other Israeli leaders that their survival depended upon good intelligence, and that a prime objective had to be the creation of the finest intelligence service in the world.

In terms of a foreign espionage and intelligence-gathering service, a network already existed throughout Europe and provided the short-term answer to Israeli needs, although a measure of selection and filtering had to take place in the new post-war situation. As far as recruits were concerned, one of the Mossad heads, Tzvi Zamir, stated that 'What the Mossad looks for are men trained to kill but with a deep aversion to killing' (Stewart Steven. *The spymasters of Israel*, p. 321). In the early days the Israeli government was stringent in what was demanded of its agents. It required 'that they be motivated by patriotism, not personal gain, that they represent the best of Israeli society, not the worst, that they obey the unique tenet of self-restraint rather than the triggermen who would glory in bloodshed, and that they remember that they are defending a democracy, not a monolithic state which ruthlessly crushes its enemies both at home and abroad' (Dan Raviv & Yossi Melman. *Every spy a prince*, p. 2). The Mossad was born out of two of the pre-independence movements, the Sha'i or Sherut Yediot and the Mossad Aliyah Beth, the former being the Haganah's secret intelligence arm and the latter the Jewish Agency for Palestine's European network. Both organizations as separate entities were professional, highly competitive and very political in terms of seeking prominence within the fledgling state. However, in 1951 Ben-Gurion decided to amalgamate the two agencies and to co-ordinate all of Israel's intelligence activities. All agencies with a military objective were formed into the IDF Military Intelligence, which is better known as Aman, and the Mossad became the other arm, that of the Secret Intelligence Services.

The structure of the Mossad and the basis for its future successes were largely laid by the first real controller, Isser Harel, who assumed command on 16 September 1952. Harel had been a counter-intelligence officer and head of Shin Beth, the domestic intelligence service; he had good administrative ability, a reputation for honesty and a flair for intelligence work. It was Harel who warned Ben-Gurion that 'A political intelligence organization without proper political

Introduction

support and resources would humiliate and one day haunt the State of Israel' (Stewart Steven. *The spymasters of Israel*, p. 43). Harel's prophecy was proved to be accurate when Shin Beth was infiltrated by Russian agents who were aides of Ben-Gurion and several espionage cases came to light. The Mossad under Harel was immune from these scandals and began to build up a reputation for ruthless efficiency and dedicated professionalism.

Israel can be regarded as unique in the degree of respect that was accorded to the intelligence services by its citizens and by other intelligence services. Indeed, a secret CIA study, released by Iran after the seizure of the US embassy in Tehran in 1979, concluded that 'Israel's intelligence and security services are amongst the best in the world. Their expert personnel and sophisticated techniques have made them highly effective, and they have demonstrated outstanding ability to organize, screen and evaluate information obtained from recruited agents, Jewish communities, and other sources throughout the world.'

The first major coup enjoyed by the Mossad was that of being the first Western intelligence service to obtain a copy of Krushchev's speech of 25 February 1956 to the Soviet Communist Party Congress, in which he denounced the Stalin era. In fact the achievement was the work of a lone Mossad maverick agent but the success personified the *esprit de corps* of the agency. Another dramatic operation took place in 1960 with the kidnapping of Adolph Eichmann from Buenos Aires in order to bring him to trial in Israel for crimes against the Jewish people and humanity. This episode attracted the attention of the world's media, as did the subsequent trial, and the reputation of the Mossad was greatly enhanced though little was really known publicly about its structure, operational capability or world-wide network.

A prime example of the effectiveness of the Israeli intelligence was the Six Day war of 1967, the triumphant outcome of which was ascribed to first-class intelligence. Much of the success of the action against Syria is directly attributable to the work of Eli Cohen, a Mossad agent operating in Damascus. Cohen was an Egyptian Jew who took on the cover of a rich, successful Syrian from Argentina. He so ingratiated himself into the higher echelons of the Ba'ath party that he became not only a trusted confidant of many of its leaders but even designate Syrian Defence Minister. Prior to his capture in 1965, Cohen provided Israel with the dispositions of the Syrian military forces and installations and, most significantly, the detailed plans of the Golan Heights defences.

This information was instrumental in the relative ease with which the Golan Plateau was captured by the Israeli Defence Forces on 9 May 1967. Coupled with this success was the Mossad's role in persuading

Introduction

an Iraqi Air Force pilot to defect with his MiG21, the acquisition of which greatly aided the Israeli Air Force in operational flying during the Six Day war. Conversely, the failure to foresee the Yom Kippur war in 1973 was seen as an aberration, even though the failure was that of the headquarters analysts and government military strategists and politicians rather than of the Mossad field agents. However, its reputation was restored by the rescue of hostages in 1978 from Entebbe airport; this operation was seized upon by the world media, thus resurrecting the image of invincibility that the Mossad enjoyed.

Between the 1967 and 1973 Arab–Israeli wars the Mossad was heavily involved in actions against Palestinian guerrillas and with Palestinian terrorist attacks on Israeli targets outside Israel. In 1968 the Popular Front for the Liberation of Palestine (PFLP) under George Habash began to launch a series of attacks against El Al aircraft and subsequently other airlines flying to Israel. The first attack was made on 23 July 1968 with the hijack of an El Al flight from Rome to Tel Aviv, and was followed by further attacks in 1968 and 1969 on El Al planes at Athens and Zurich. On 29 August 1969 there was another hijacking, this time of a TWA flight from Rome to Tel Aviv. These actions escalated on 6 September 1970 with the hijacking of four aircraft en route to Tel Aviv; three were flown to Dawson's airfield in the Jordanian desert and the fourth to Cairo. The Jordanian episode turned out to be a disaster for the Palestinians, however, as the Jordanian army attacked Palestinian bases within Jordan, causing the Palestinians to seek refuge in Lebanon. The episode became known in Palestinian circles as 'Black September'.

This event gave birth to the Black September organization which became one of the most feared terrorist groups in the world at that time. Initially its wrath was directed against Jordan but it soon turned its attention to attacks upon Israeli targets. Although the Palestine Liberation Organization (PLO) claimed that it did not control Black September, it had in fact been formed secretly by Yasser Arafat and led by his deputy Abu Iyad as a vehicle to wage war on the enemies of the Palestinians without tarnishing the image of the PLO.

A number of offences took place against Israeli, or pro-Israeli targets, with attacks on Dutch oil tanks in the Netherlands, aircraft en route to Israel and the massacre at Lod International Airport on 30 May 1972 by members of the Japanese Red Army acting on behalf of Black September. The massacre left twenty-seven people dead and seventy seriously injured, and demonstrated the extent to which the Palestinians were now part of an international network.

Black September's most infamous European operation was the murder of nine Israeli athletes at the 1972 Munich Olympic Games.

Introduction

The Israeli hostages were taken on 6 September but the Bavarian police were not really equipped to handle the crisis; during a stand-off at Fürstenfeldbrück airfield, a policeman opened fire and in the resultant action all nine Israeli hostages were killed. The episode was regarded by the Palestinians as a great victory and in an interview on 13 September 1972 Habash stated that 'The choice of the Olympics, from a purely propagandist viewpoint, was 100 per cent successful. It was like painting the name of Palestine on a mountain that can be seen from the four corners of the earth' (As-Sayyid, 13 September 1972 [in Arabic]; also in D. Hirst. *The gun and the olive branch*, p. 314).

The Munich massacre was followed by a series of letter bomb attacks which began on 18 September 1972; seventy letter bombs were sent from Amsterdam to Israeli targets throughout the world, although only the Agricultural Attaché at the London embassy was killed. This was followed on 4 October by a further series of letter bombs sent from Malaysia and then on 25 October by letter bombs to the US President, the Secretary of State and Defense Secretary, mailed from Israel by sleeper agents. Over a period of four years Black September had waged unremitting war against Israel.

The campaign by Black September and its allies forced the Mossad and Shin Beth to divert resources to counter the problem. They did meet with some initial success; Shin Beth, for example, almost eliminated the El Al hijacking risk. The Mossad directed its attention against terrorist capabilities in the Middle East and Europe, with increased espionage activity against Arab states and the Palestine liberation movements. Mossad agents were also placed in El Al offices to supervise security checks in airports and the interrogation of suspicious travellers; in this they enjoyed a measure of success. Further successes were recorded by the Mossad in Europe, especially through the station chief in Brussels, Baruch Cohen, who provided valuable intelligence on the PFLP recruitment of unsuspecting female Europeans, the identification of the European controller of the PFLP, Mohammad Boudia, and links between the Palestinians and other terrorist factions such as Baader-Meinhoff. However, the intelligence gained, although impressive, did not stop the incidents and failed to address the question of what to do about the terrorists.

A large section of the military and many politicians advocated the assassination of the Palestinian leadership as the only effective deterrent. This was a particularly sensitive issue within Israel as it was felt that such a policy would lead to a lowering of the standards of morality. The massacre at Lod International Airport, however, caused a change in Israeli public opinion. This led to the Mossad controller responding by carrying out assassination attempts on key targets, such as the car bomb attack on Ghassan Kanafari, a member of the PFLP's Central Command, and one of the planners behind the Lod airport massacre.

Following the Munich massacre, the Prime Minister, Golda Meir, created the post of Special Adviser for Terrorist Matters and appointed Major-General Yariv to the post. He formed a good working relationship with the head of Mossad, Zamir. The new policy was designed to target the planning strategists of the Palestinian movements and field operatives rather than the political leadership of the PLO. The policy was not a licence for the Mossad to operate indiscriminately as all operations had to be approved by a secret tribunal consisting of the Prime Minister, Defence Minister and Foreign Minister.

A number of highly emotive newspaper accounts talked about 'hit teams' or 'assassination squads' roaming Europe and the Middle East in the search for Palestinian terrorists. In reality, the operations were more likely to have been carried out by teams of agents who were experts in the country of operation and probably drawn from intelligence, security and military units. In his book *Language of violence: the blood politics of terrorism*, Edward O'Ballance concluded that two separate teams were involved in each action, with an assassination team and a diversionary and escape unit working through Israeli embassies, El Al and Zim shipping offices.

The campaign was waged with increasing violence on both sides until eventually the Mossad broke the power of Black September. However, the change in policy had led to problems as Mossad operations in Europe were often at variance with agreed procedures for co-operation with other security services. An example of this was the Sowan affair in 1987, when the Mossad agent, Sowan, was arrested in Britain and the sheer volume of activity in the country was disclosed; this resulted in Sowan being imprisoned and five Israeli embassy staff being expelled. British tolerance was further strained by Mossad complicity in the kidnappings of the Nigerian official Omaru Diku and Mordechai Vananu and the discovery of forged British passports for use by the Mossad. The affair was equivalent, in terms of relationships, to the Pollard case in the United States.

The 1980s saw a series of events which almost totally destroyed the morale of Israeli intelligence, especially, though not exclusively, the Mossad. The first incident was the Israeli invasion of Lebanon in 1982 which succeeded in forcing out the Palestinian guerrillas but which then went awry, with major misjudgements being made by the Mossad. The Israelis had opened secret contact with the Christians in the belief that this would secure Israel's borders, but it proved to be an error of

Introduction

judgement. The Mossad failed to use its intelligence to prevent or ameliorate the resultant political disaster. In fact, the whole operation was considered a political disaster: it caused disorders within Israel, damaged Israel's world-wide interests, failed in the objective of destroying the PLO, left Lebanon in a state of anarchy, and provided support for the Hezbellah movement in its actions against Israel. The close relationship between the Mossad agents in Lebanon and the Phalange leader Bashir Gemayel also meant that Israel became tainted by the massacres at the refugee camps of Shatilla and Sabra. Mossad dealings with the Christians were ill judged and drew the Mossad agents into the very unsavoury inter-community activities between the Christians and the Muslims, for many of these activities were criminal in nature and aimed at personal accrual of wealth and power rather than the objectives of a just cause. Israeli public opinion was also divided on the merits of the Lebanese invasion and the wisdom of attempted occupation of the southern section of the country so that when Israeli military deaths resulted a section of the public actively campaigned for Israeli withdrawal.

Relations with the United States were also put under strain by the Jonathan Jay Pollard case in 1984. Pollard, who was employed by United States Naval Intelligence, volunteered to work for Israel, though the Mossad subsequently insisted that he take payment for his services. The Mossad was anxious to obtain intelligence on the Arab capability for nuclear and chemical warfare and charged Pollard with providing this information. In addition, Pollard provided information regarding the air defence capabilities of Libya, Tunisia and Algeria, and this was used by Israel for a raid on the PLO in Tunis following the murder of Israeli citizens in Larnaca, Cyprus.

The exposure of Pollard was a major blow to US–Israeli relations although the Israeli government attempted to limit the damage by claiming that it was a rogue operation which got out of control. However, investigations within Israel showed that all the armed forces had provided Pollard with a list of requirements which indicated that the operation had some measure of official sanction. Although the US–Israeli relationship was unlikely to be terminated by the episode, it was a major embarrassment to both governments and also provoked a critical examination within Israel of the Mossad and other intelligence agencies.

Nor was the reputation of Mossad enhanced by its involvement in the Iran–Contra affair, since Israel's reputation was already sullied by the political backlash arising from the affair in the United States and by the disclosure of Israel's involvement with Iran even during the period of the Khomeini revolution and the Iran–Iraq war. It seemed as

Introduction

if the Mossad and Israeli intelligence in general was subject to a series of failures and setbacks which followed in quick succession. Amongst these were the interception of a Libyan jet in the mistaken belief that it carried Palestinian terrorists, the expulsion of double agents from Britain, the clumsy and ill-timed kidnapping of the nuclear informer Mordechai Vananu, and the failure to warn the government of problems in the occupied territories prior to the Intifada. The Mossad had also been charged with identifying the extent of Iraq's military build-up, particularly in the nuclear field; hence the raid on her nuclear reactor in 1981. As a result of this activity the Mossad is thought to have been heavily involved in the investigation of the Iraqi 'supergun' and the murder in Belgium of its developer Gerald Bull on 22 March 1990. Finally, the Mossad seemed to have lost control of its freelance agents throughout the world and was still trying to preserve an outdated censorship system at a time when questions were being asked in Israel about the activities, effectiveness and accountability of the intelligence services.

In company with other branches of the intelligence service, the Mossad suffered from a crisis of confidence as, instead of being able to account publicly for its actions, there were concerted efforts to leave any questions unanswered. The charge of identified brutality, torture and perjury by Shin Beth was established by a commission of inquiry, but no one admitted giving the orders for killing the prisoners and although the leader of Shin Beth resigned, the politicians were not held accountable. Inevitably, all the intelligence agencies were tarnished by these findings.

Irangate blew up in 1986. The United States government attempted to blame Israel, by claiming manipulation by the Mossad of both the Iranians and Americans to suit Israel's own needs. In reality, the Mossad had been opposed to the attempt to swap arms for hostages, but as its controller was so low in the bureaucratic pecking order, he was unable to prevent Israeli participation.

By the beginnings of the 1990s an intelligence service which had once been very secretive and highly respected had become better known and subject to criticism and disillusionment. Nevertheless, it is inevitable that clandestine operations will still be kept secret by the Mossad and the Israeli government, even when successful. Indeed, it should be noted that it was the failures which generally became known and the subject of criticism. It could also be argued that a country's intelligence service is merely a reflection of the society and that its structure and behaviour are shaped by that country's society.

However, David Kimche, a former deputy director of Mossad, claimed in 1987 that the agency was in decline and that the calibre of

Introduction

staff had fallen. 'The main difference was the great motivation of our people. It was a matter of mission and readiness to work day and night with unlimited dedication' (*Yediot Aharonat* [Tel Aviv], January 1987, p. 2, 9, 16). A counter-view was the prediction by Isser Harel, the second head of the Mossad, who said in relation to Mossad's reputation that 'They should stop spinning legends around Mossad. I think that we just work harder and collect more information than the others. No other country in the world has such urgent need for an efficient secret service. Israel is surrounded by enemies. We have no diplomatic relations with those nations whose agents clobber us as terrorists. For us it is a question of survival' (R. Payne. *Mossad: Israel's most secret service*, p. 6).

Notwithstanding this, the existence of the Mossad has also been valuable as an alternative diplomatic service, liaising with countries who were not prepared to deal openly with Israel, or when the Foreign Ministry at times caused rivalry and mistrust between the unofficial and official diplomats. In some cases the Mossad subcontracted these liaisons to freelance or former agents as fiefdoms, but the organization had been instrumental in opening hitherto closed doors and maintaining relations with countries that did not wish to admit such dealings. A link through the Mossad gave the recipient country an easy way out for the receipt of military, agricultural, medical and economic aid without risking a boycott from the Arab world. In this context China, Indonesia and Morocco have been involved through the Mossad, which has also provided training for intelligence services in South America and Africa.

One such link which has now become public was with Ethiopia, which resumed normal ties in November 1989 as a result of years of patient work by Mossad agents. The link brought several benefits: the resettling of Ethiopian Jews left behind after the conclusion of the secret exodus; the re-establishment of an Israeli listening-post on the Red Sea which could monitor traffic to and from Saudi Arabia, Jordan, Sudan and Egypt; and a convenient Mossad base within the Israeli embassy in Addis Ababa. In return, the Ethiopian government obtained agricultural assistance and expertise, and training in guerrilla warfare.

The situation in the Middle East is in a state of flux, with a delicate peace process under way with the Palestinians – the process is continuing at the time of writing despite the murder of Prime Minister Rabin and the uncertain position of Shimon Peres. In addition, Israel has concluded a peace treaty with Jordan, and negotiations are still in being with Syria though these are subject to fundamental problems over the Golan Heights. There is little doubt that the Mossad will now be co-operating with their opposite numbers in Egypt and Jordan

Introduction

against the common threat posed by the Islamic Fundamentalists and attempting to counter any threats to Israel or to regimes in the Middle East sympathetic to Israel's survival. There is little doubt that the work of the Mossad, its predecessors and allied agencies have contributed greatly to the survival of Israel as a state.

About the bibliography

A large amount of the preliminary work on this bibliography was undertaken during a research visit to the Russell J. Bowen Collection on Intelligence, Security and Covert Activities in the Lauinger Library at Georgetown University, Washington DC. In this respect I owe a debt of gratitude to the Special Collections Librarian, Marty Ballinger for his assistance, particularly with uncatalogued material, and for allowing me access whilst the library was officially closed for building works.

The work aims to provide a representative coverage of the available material, primarily in the English language. For this reason, some rather short items are included because they reflect the nature of one significant section of the published material on the Mossad. However, a large number of speculative works have been omitted because of their questionable nature in terms of accuracy and relevance.

A large number of sources are, of course, unavailable because of the nature of the subject matter and, moreover, much of the official material is only available in Hebrew. Some of these sources are, however, covered in this introduction and I am indebted to my colleague, Shlomo Shpiro, for information on Hebrew sources on the Mossad and Israeli intelligence generally.

As in most Western countries, the archives of the intelligence services are restricted to internal use and the thirty-year rule for the release of documents in Israel does not apply to this material. However, two categories of primary sources exist which are invaluable for research on Israeli intelligence.

The first category covers the various judicial commissions of investigation established to explore intelligence failures. A number of commissions were set up, headed by a supreme court judge, with powers to review the documents and summon intelligence personnel as witnesses to investigate various intelligence failures. English-language material available on these reports is included in the bibliography but the originals are in Hebrew and lodged in the Israeli State Archives in Jerusalem. Amongst these commissions are: the Agranat Commission set up to investigate the intelligence failures of the Yom Kippur War; the Landau Commission on the use of physical

Introduction

interrogation techniques by the Shabak; and the Shamgar Commission on the failure to prevent the assassination of Prime Minister Rabin. Limited sections of these reports are still secret but they provide nonetheless a deep and probing official examination of the activities of the Mossad and the other intelligence services.

The second category of primary material is the collection of Hazav intelligence reports which are housed in the Moshe Dayan Centre for Middle Eastern Studies in Tel-Aviv University. Hazav is a unit within Aman which monitors all open sources in Arab countries, covering newspapers, radio and television broadcasts, political statements and communiqués, and producing reports which are distributed within government and political circles. The reports from 1950 onwards comprise hundreds of volumes with over a quarter of a million documents which are available to the public. A series of daily reports is available from 1962, but in 1987 the series was divided into two, with a daily report series dealing with political intelligence, and a second dealing with economic, social, and infrastructure intelligence.

The reports from Hazav are the only official Israeli intelligence reports available for research and they also provide a valuable indication of the priorities of the intelligence collection efforts in specific periods and on specific issues. As these reports were available to the policy-makers they also demonstrate the threat perceptions and images which influenced the political decisions and military actions of Israeli leaders.

Various aspects of intelligence and other issues are also dealt with in three offcial Israeli publications. *Bamahane* is the weekly magazine of the Israeli army which has been published regularly since 1948. Although it primarily features articles on army activities, unit profiles, and documentary reports, special issues regularly cover intelligence topics such as radio interception and the use of spy drones. *Skira Hodshit* is a monthly magazine for Israeli army officers which, whilst dealing with military issues, concentrates on political and economic issues in other countries, notably the Arab states. Many articles contain references to Arab intelligence activities, terrorism, and other related matters, written by academics and intended to give Israeli officers a wider knowledge than professional military issues.

Academic studies of the Israeli intelligence services have developed slowly outside of the Mossad Academy and the Israeli National Security College, both of which are restricted to senior active government officials. Collections in university libraries are severely limited, though one library does specialize in intelligence issues. This is the Malam library which is located at the Centre for the Commemoration of the Fallen among the intelligence community, offering a unique collection of books, many available only in Hebrew. The library is affiliated to Aman but the public can gain admission by appointment with enquiries to be sent to the Malam Library, Military Post 02785, Israel. Adjacent to the library is a large memorial engraved with the names of hundreds of intelligence officers and agents killed on duty in numerous wars or on covert activities.

As a general rule former Israeli intelligence officers are prohibited from publishing their memoirs and most requests are denied by the military censor. Books sanctioned for publication were passed only after references to serving or former intelligence operatives had been removed, except for former heads of services whose names were in the public domain.

The most prolific intelligence writer in Israel is the former head of the Mossad, Isser Harel, and his works in English, or in translation, are included in this bibliography. However, his most comprehensive work, *Bitachan veDemocratia* (Security and democracy) (Tel-Aviv: Idanim, 1989), is only available in Hebrew. It covers the first two decades of Israeli intelligence activities against the background of the role of the intelligence services within a democracy, and includes details on Israel's intelligence co-operation with Western states.

A large amount of Hebrew literature on intelligence deals with activities prior to the establishment of the Israeli state in 1948, primarily because it was easier to obtain approval for such publications. However, these publications provide useful information on intelligence officers who later became part of the Mossad, Shin Beth or Aman. An example of this type of work is Efraim Dekel's *Alilot Shay* (The story of Shai) (Tel-Aviv: Ma'archat, 1953), written by a former Haganah operative who became involved in the secret services of the new state.

Due to the censorship regulations imposed on former members of the intelligence community, a trend has developed where journalists or writers publish books based on intensive interviews with former operatives. The sources of these books are not acknowledged but the content is such that it could only have come from people intimately involved in the relevant operations. Two recent books in Hebrew are Yosef Argaman's *Ze Haya Sodi Beyoter* (This was top secret) (Tel-Aviv: Israel Ministry of Defence Publications, 1990), and Yizhack Shoshan's *Anshei Hasod veHaseter* (People of secrets) (Tel-Aviv: Idanim, 1990). Both books provide detailed information on various intelligence activities based on inside knowledge.

In addition to the official investigations, intelligence failures have also been the subject of several books. In particular, the capture of

Introduction

the Israeli covert network in Egypt during the early 1950s, known as the *Parasha* affair, and the failure of the intelligence services to warn of the impending Yom Kippur War in 1973. Both of these events had major political repercussions in Israel and several different and contradictory accounts of these events have been published.

The earliest book on the *Parasha* is Dan Horowitz's and Eliyahu Hasin's *HaParasha* (The affair) (Tel-Aviv: Am HaSefer, 1961). At the time of publication many details of the affair were still secret and several of the captured agents still in Egyptian prisons. The surviving agents were released in 1967 and recount their experiences in Aviezer Golan's *Mivza Susanna* (Operation Susanna) (Jerusalem: Idanim, 1976). The intelligence concepts which brought about the operation are dealt with in Hagai Eshed's *Mi Natan Et HaHora'a* (Who gave the order) (Jerusalem: Idanim, 1979), whilst Yosef Almogi's *HaMa'avak Al Ben Gurion* (The struggle over Ben Gurion) (Tel-Aviv: Idanim, 1988) examines the grave political repercussions that the affair had on Israeli politics and on Prime Minister Ben-Gurion. The most recent book on this affair, written by Professor Yehoshafat Harkabi, former head of Aman, *Edut Ishit* (Personal statement) (Tel-Aviv: Ramot, 1994), recounts his personal involvement with the *Parasha* affair.

The attack by the Arab armies in 1973 on Israel, resulting in the Yom Kippur or Ramadan War, shook the whole of the Israeli intelligence community and there are several English-language items in this bibliography on this subject. Shlomo Nakdiomn's *Svirut Nemucha* (Low probability) (Tel-Aviv: Revivim, 1982) is the most comprehensive account of the failure of Aman to provide early warning of Egyptian military intentions. This is also covered by Yoel Ben-Porat's *Neila* (Last prayer) (Tel-Aviv: Idanim, 1991) who was the head of Aman's Central Warning Unit at the outbreak of the war. A recent addition to the literature is Eli Zeira's *Milhemet Yom haKipurum: Mitos Mul Meziut* (The Yom Kippur War: myth against reality) (Tel-Aviv: Yediot Acharonot, 1993). Zeira was a former Aman commander who was held by many to be responsible for the intelligence débâcle and this work represents an attempt to redress the accusation levelled against him by the Agranat report and to dispel the myth that the military action was a surprise.

The peace process in the Middle East is gradually changing the veil of secrecy which traditionally covered the Israeli intelligence services. The ban on the naming of the Mossad and Shin Beth heads of services has been lifted and their public appearance in forums and discussions on security may signal more openness in the future. If the strict censorship regulations governing the publication of memoirs

Introduction

and books by former intelligence officers are relaxed more authoritative studies may emerge.

A wealth of relevant material providing background information to personalities and events also exists but has been excluded because they contain no direct references to the Mossad and would have distorted the balance of the work. To have included them would have meant citing practically every title on the Palestinian question, the Arab-Israeli wars, and contemporary Lebanese history as the Mossad would have had an input to the intelligence aspects of all of these areas. It is therefore essential for the researcher to read into wider areas in order to fully appreciate the significant role played by the Israeli Intelligence Services in general, and the Mossad in particular.

Intelligence Services: General Works

1 **Beirut spy.**
   Said K. Aburish.   London: Bloomsbury Publishing, 1990. 214p.

An account, by a journalist, of people and events associated with the bar of the St George Hotel in Beirut from the early 1950s to the mid-1990s. This is a collection of anecdotes about a major focal point of international intrigue in the Middle East when spies, politicians, businessmen, journalists and oil sheikhs treated the bar as an informal club and as a centre for information exchange. Personalities associated with the Mossad form part of this coverage which is aimed at the general reader.

2 **Merchants of treason: America's secrets for sale. From the Pueblo to the present.**
   Thomas B. Allen, Norman Palmer.   New York: Delacote Press, 1988. 378p. bibliog.

Allen and Palmer make a detailed analysis of Soviet-bloc, Israeli and other foreign espionage successes in the United States and the failure of US counter-intelligence agencies. The emphasis is on the period 1978-88 and there are numerous references to operations of the Mossad. The work is based on interviews and published sources. It includes a chronology of United States espionage cases between 1953 and 1987, and a glossary of terms.

3 **The dictionary of espionage: spookspeak into English.**
   Henry S. A. Becket.   New York: Stein, 1986. 203p.

An explanation of words used in the espionage area, known as tradecraft. Some 2,000 words are translated into plain English. Amongst agencies covered are MI5, the CIA, France's DGSE and the Mossad.

Intelligence Services: General Works

4   **Greatest spies and spymasters.**
    Roger Boar, Nigel Blundell.   London: Octopus Books, 1984. 192p.

This illustrated account of noted spymasters and spies is aimed at the general reader and contains only sketchy information on each entry. Of relevance to the Mossad are those on Eli Cohen, Wolfgang Lotz, and the kidnap and trial of Adolf Eichmann.

5   **Spy/counterspy: an encyclopaedia of espionage.**
    Vincent Buranelli, Nan Buranelli.   London; New York: McGraw Hill, 1982. 361p. bibliog.

A series of one-page entries on spying organizations, including the Mossad, individual personalities and techniques, together with significant cases throughout history.

6   **'C': a biography of Sir Maurice Oldfield, Head of MI6.**
    Richard Deacon [pseudonym of Donald McCormick].   London: Macdonald & Co., 1985. 279p.

Much wider in coverage than the Middle East but the period when Oldfield was head of MI6 (1975-78) does deal with the role of intelligence services in the region. There are numerous implicit and explicit references to the Mossad.

7   **Spyclopaedia: the comprehensive handbook of espionage.**
    Richard Deacon [pseud].   London: Macdonald & Co., 1988. 416p.

Deacon's compilation, aimed at the general reader, gives short accounts of spies, secret services, intelligence organizations and subjects related to the field of espionage. The work falls into three parts: spies from 510 BC to AD 1781; spies from 1914 to 1945; and spies from 1946 to 1987. Israel is part of the coverage and the Mossad is included in this broad account.

8   **War without end; the terrorists: an intelligence dossier.**
    Christopher Dobson, Ronald Payne.   London: Harrap, 1986. 279p. bibliog.

A detailed examination of contemporary international terrorism, including the Middle East. It includes consideration of the infrastructure, personalities, objectives and tactics of various Palestinian and Shi'ite groups and the role of the Mossad in countering their activities. The appendices contain details of terrorist organizations and provide a chronology of terrorist events.

9   **The future of espionage.**
    Queens Quarterly, vol. 100 (Summer 1993), p. 269-414. maps. bibliog.

Discusses the impact of intelligence and spying on Western culture, covering both national and international aspects of the subject. Amongst the organizations discussed are MI5, the former East Germany's Stasi, and the Mossad.

10   **The road to peace: a biography of Shimon Peres.**
    Matti Golan.   New York: Warner Books, 1989. 357p. bibliog.

This biography of Shimon Peres by an Israeli journalist uses material in Peres' private papers and his own eyewitness experience. In relation to the Mossad, the chapter

Intelligence Services: General Works

entitled 'On the way to leadership' (p. 113-64) deals extensively with the Entebbe operation and the role of the organization in negotiations with Kenya to facilitate an Israeli raid to free the hostages.

11 Ben-Gurion: prophet of fire.
Don Kurzman. New York: Simon & Schuster, 1983. 544p. bibliog.

Kurzman's authoritative biography of Ben-Gurion largely concentrates on his role in the foundation and early leadership of the State of Israel. The work is based on extensive interviews, archival research, and an examination of Ben-Gurion's unpublished diaries and letters. There are references to the organization of illegal immigration into Palestine, the origins of the Mossad, and the intelligence dilemmas of the Yom Kippur war.

12 The age of terrorism.
Walter Laqueur. Boston, Massachusetts: Little, Brown & Co., 1987. 385p. bibliog.

A revision of the author's previous work, entitled *Terrorism*, which provides a scholarly study of political terror from its roots in early nineteenth-century Europe to the 1980s. Laqueur examines, amongst other topics, the sociology of terror, intelligence gathering, counter-terrorism, and the role of the media. He also deals with Abu Nidal, Al Fatah, George Habash, the Palestine Liberation Organization, Libyan terrorism and relations between Iran and Israel. The Munich Olympic Games massacre is also covered, as is the role of the Mossad in hunting those responsible.

13 A world of secrets: the uses and limits of intelligence.
Walter Laqueur. London: Weidenfeld & Nicolson; New York: Basic Books, 1985. 404p. bibliog.

This work is primarily concerned with United States intelligence activities since the Second World War. The author provides a critical overview and assessment of activities, including relations between the CIA and the Mossad.

14 Intelligence and strategic surprises.
Ariel Levite. New York: Columbia Press, 1987. 220p.

This is a scholarly analysis of the basic nature of strategic surprise and its relationship to policy-making which points up the crucial need for high-quality intelligence warnings to overcome normal bureaucratic inertia. The work concentrates largely on Pearl Harbor and Midway as case-studies. However, the author was a former Israeli Defence officer and Ministry of Defence analyst and he also deals with the Yom Kippur (or Ramadan) war of 1973, in relation to the differing views of Israeli Military Intelligence and the Mossad over the interpretation of data prior to the Egyptian and Syrian attacks. The author demonstrates how the intelligence data from Egypt and Syria was received with differing views by the two branches of intelligence and the Israeli politicians, and relates this to the main theme of the book.

Intelligence Services: General Works

15 The war against terrorism.
Neil C. Livingstone. Lexington, Massachusetts: Lexington Books, 1982. 291p.

A scholarly, authoritative review of modern international terrorism and counter-terrorism. Amongst other topics, the work considers Al Fatah, Black September, George Habash, the Lebanon, Arab front-line states, the Palestine Liberation Organization, Libya and the Munich Olympic Games massacre. In terms of Israel the intelligence and counter-terrorism agencies are considered as is the role of the Mossad, particularly in relation to the Olympic Games massacre.

16 The Sphynx of Damascus: a political biography.
Moshe Asad Ma'oz. London; New York: Weidenfeld & Nicolson, 1988. 226p. bibliog.

A political biography of President Hafiz al-Asad of Syria from 1970. Asad is seen as a shrewd, charismatic strongman who dreamt of the unification of the Arab world under the banner of a Greater Syria. The work reviews Asad's actions and techniques from astute diplomacy and double-dealing to military intervention and state terrorism, and describes the central role of the President's minority sect, the Alawis, in Syria's intelligence and security forces. Also covered are the activities of Israeli intelligence agencies, including Mossad, in intelligence gathering, espionage and counter-espionage, together with consideration of Al Fatah, Abu Nidal, and the Palestine Liberation Organization.

17 Crossroads of modern warfare: sixteen twentieth century battles that shaped contemporary history.
Drew Middleton. New York: Doubleday & Co., 1983. 320p. bibliog.

Middleton reviews sixteen modern battles, with the emphasis on the intelligence aspects. The Yom Kippur war is considered as one of the significant military actions and there are numerous references to the Palestine Liberation Organization and the Mossad.

18 Warriors of the night: spies, soldiers and American intelligence.
Ernest Nolkman. New York: William Morrow & Co., 1985. 443p. bibliog.

This is a detailed review of Western, particularly United States, intelligence failures since the First World War, written by an investigative journalist. The work is based on interviews and secondary sources and includes references to the Mossad.

19 Foreign intelligence organizations.
Jeffrey T. Richelson. Cambridge, Massachusetts: Ballinger Publishing Co., 1988. 330p.

A detailed compendium of the intelligence and security organizations, capabilities and operations of a number of states. It covers Israel, the Palestinians, Libya, Syria, the Middle East in general and, specifically, the Six Day and Yom Kippur wars. The latter is specifically relevant for the success of the Arab misinformation propaganda which was wrongly interpreted by Israeli Military Intelligence, correctly by the Mossad, and indecision by Israeli politicians.

Intelligence Services: General Works

20 For lust of knowing: memoirs of an intelligence officer.
Archibald Bulloch Roosevelt. London: Weidenfeld & Nicolson, 1987. 500p. bibliog.

This is a highly informative, first-class series of recollections from a retired intelligence officer specializing in the Middle East. The author was an accomplished linguist with a passionate interest in Islamic culture. The work provides a running in-depth, authoritative account of the history, politics, sociology, personalities and events of the region. As such, there is a great deal of information on the Israeli intelligence services, including the Mossad, Palestinian guerrillas, and the response of the Mossad to the activities of the Popular Front for the Liberation of Palestine and Black September. The author is also highly critical of the failure of United States policy-makers to distinguish between Islamic nationalism, long-term Islamic fundamentalism, or short-term Marxist expediency as policy issues in the region. The book is based on copious personal notes and recollections.

21 Alchemists of revolution: terrorism in the modern world.
Richard E. Rubenstein. New York: Basic Books, 1987. 266p.

Rubenstein's general review of terrorism in the modern world explores the relationship between terrorism and social revolutions, tracing its origins to nineteenth-century anarchism. The work has numerous incidental references to the Palestine Liberation Organization, Menachen Begin, Islamic Jihad, the Mossad and other secret service and terrorism organizations.

22 The intelligence game: illusions and delusion of international espionage.
James Rusbridger. London: Bodley Head, 1989. 278p.

A controversial examination of the international intelligence business which argues that their activities are cloaked in secrecy mainly to conceal their lack of effectiveness. All are deemed guilty of propagating mythical enemies to fuel the paranoia of their political masters and to provide mutual support. The work is largely concerned with MI5 and MI6, but also covers the Israeli intelligence services, including the Mossad. This is a highly cynical account, based on public and private records, and on interviews with individuals in Israel and other countries.

23 A history of Israel: from the rise of Zionism to our time.
Howard M. Sachar. New York: Alfred A. Knopf, 1979. 887p. maps. bibliog.

Sacher's authoritative history of Israel to the late 1970s provides a useful backcloth to contemporary situations. In terms of the Mossad the only specific references are to the Yom Kippur war and the differences between Military Intelligence and the Mossad over the interpretation of intelligence data from Egypt and Israel.

24 To win or die: a personal narrative of Menachin Begin.
N. Temko. New York: William Morrow, 1987. 460p. bibliog.

A detailed biography of Menachin Begin, with an emphasis on his early leadership of the Jewish underground movements and his subsequent forceful leadership of Israel. Based on extensive interviews and unpublished sources with references to Yasser Arafat, the Palestine Liberation Organization, the nuclear reactor raid on Iraq

Intelligence Services: General Works

organized by the Mossad, and the Yom Kippur war with its associated disinformation campaign waged by the Arabs.

25 **Ben-Gurion: the burning ground 1886-1948.**
    Shabtai Teveth.   Boston, Massachusetts: Houghton Mifflin, 1987. 967p. bibliog.

A scholarly biography of David Ben-Gurion leading to the creation of the State of Israel in 1948. The illustrated work has many references to Jewish underground activity and the development of the Mossad.

26 **The rescuers: the world top anti-terrorist units.**
    Leroy Thompson.   Boulder, Colorado: Paladin Press, 1986. 241p.

Thompson surveys the major counter-terrorism forces of the Free World, including the Mossad, and special units of the Israeli Defence Forces. He covers weapons, equipment, and training, and provides a summary of major terrorist actions and terrorists groups, including the various Palestinian factions.

27 **The secrets of a spymaster: East Germany's top spook talks about his craft.**
    Theresa Waldrop, Karen Breslau.   *Newsweek*, vol. 118, no. 21 (18 Nov. 1991), p. 42.

An interview with Markus Wolf, former head of the East German Intelligence service between 1958 and 1987. It covers the successes of his spying operations and includes a consideration of the Mossad.

28 **Games of intelligence: the classified conflict of international espionage.**
    Nigel West.   London: Hodder & Stoughton, 1989. 248p.

This work is a review and comparison of six of the major intelligence services based on a survey of the available literature. The services considered are the United States CIA, the Soviet Union KGB and GRU, France's DGSE, the United Kingdom's Secret Intelligence Services, and Israel's Mossad. The criteria used in the assessment of their effectiveness are: integrity of services; operational prowess; and product exploitation. The Mossad is dealt with in Chapter 8 'The Institute' (p. 171-92) and is considered overall to be a very close second across all measured criteria to the Soviet Union's GRU or Military Intelligence. There are other minor references to the Mossad in other sections where there were known links with specified operations or events.

29 **Vital intelligence: a nation's right.**
    Emanuel A. Winston.   *Midstream*, vol. 33 (June/July 1987), p. 9-10.

A discussion of United States and Israeli intelligence services which argues that Israel, through the Mossad, was justified in accepting secrets of US defence technology from Jay Pollard. The latter was arrested and imprisoned for espionage.

Israeli Intelligence: General

30 **The Agronat Report: a partial report by the Commission of Inquiry to the Government of Israel.**
State of Israel: Government Printing Office, 1974. (In Hebrew).
This report into the performance of Aman and the Mossad was a direct result of the perceived intelligence failures of the Yom Kippur war. Recommendations of the Committee resulted in reforms within the Mossad.

31 **The Israeli special services: instruments of aggression and terror.**
V. Bashkin. *Mirovaia Ekonomika I Mezhdunarodyne Ostrosheniia*, vol. 1 (1985), p. 142-5.
Bashkin discusses the range of intelligence and security services in Israel since independence, including a consideration of the Mossad. He considers that they have played an important part in the Arab–Israeli wars and in activities against Israel's Arab neighbours and Palestinian organizations.

32 **Israel's secret wars: the untold story of Israeli intelligence.**
Ian Black, Benny Morris. London: Hamish Hamilton, 1991. 603p. bibliog.
This work is concerned with more than the Mossad but the organization does receive extensive coverage. It is based, for the period before 1960, on documentary materials available in Israeli, British and United States archives but after that date more reliance is placed upon interviews with former Israeli agents and other source material. This is not a book of revelations, nor is there much new that is revealed, but it is a carefully documented history based on verifiable evidence and related to the strategic, political, and administrative framework within which the various services operate. The book was also processed 'through the sieve of Israeli military censorship' and various appeals procedures, but the authors maintain that little has been deleted. The Israeli intelligence services are basically divided into three main sections: Aman which is the intelligence arm of the armed forces; Shin Beth which is responsible for internal security and the countering of extremist and subversive movements within Israel; and

the Mossad which is primarily charged with responsibility for foreign intelligence. However, Israel was no different from other countries in that the various agencies were still affected by inter-agency squabbles, bureaucratic rivalry, and suspicions, with lines of demarcation often ignored. The authors conclude that the major successes of Israeli intelligence have been due more to technological skills rather than those of individual agents, excellent research and analysis, and a flexible, efficient organization. One major area in which all these attributes came together was in the area of illegal immigration into Palestine which had its origins in the Mossad Aliyah Beth and involvement in the movement of European Jews from Germany and other Nazi-occupied territories. Other similar operations were mounted in Morocco, Egypt and Tunisia between 1955 and 1961, and, more recently, the Falashas, the black Jews from Ethiopia. The authors regard the capture of an Iraqi MiG 21 fighter aircraft in 1967 as 'one of the most complex and brilliant operations ever mounted by the Mossad' which crucially contributed to the Israeli victory over the Arab air forces on 5 June 1967. Subsequent operations, including the Entebbe rescue operation and the intelligence behind the identification and bombing of the Ossirak nuclear reactor in Iraq in June 1981, are cited as further successful operations which lent Israeli intelligence an air of omniscience and a public reputation and self-confidence which was not without its pitfalls. Despite these successes the 1970s and 1980s saw a series of blunders which tarnished this image. Particularly highlighted is the failure of the intelligence agencies at the outbreak of the Yom Kippur war to interpret data obtained from Egypt showing that an attack was imminent. The military, represented by Aman, believed the Egyptian build-up to be fear of an Israeli attack, although Mossad had received advance warning of an impending attack from an agent in Egypt, described later as 'the best agent any country ever had in wartime, a miraculous source'. The Mossad's reputation was further tarnished by the Jonathan Jay Pollard espionage trial in the United States on charges of spying for Israel and passing information to the Mossad, though the Israeli authorities tried to disguise it as a rogue operation. In more recent times the Mossad was involved from 1988 in a major campaign to frustrate Iraq's weapon procurement programme through direct and indirect action, and the provision of information about developments in Iraq to other Western intelligence agencies. Mossad was also believed, in some quarters, to be responsible for the murder of Gerald Bull on 22 March 1990 in Belgium because of his involvement in the development of the Iraqi 'supergun' and other weapons procurement. It is also believed that the Mossad had operated a covert operation to assassinate Abu Iyad, deputy head of Fatah, on 16 January 1991 using Hamza Abu Zid, a member of the Abu Nidal group, who thought he was acting on behalf of the group whereas he was responding to a secret Israeli directive. This could have been a 'false-flag' operation though the Palestinians have never tried to claim it as such. This is an important book which is likely to remain one of the definitive studies on Israeli intelligence.

33 **The survival factor: Israeli intelligence from World War I to the present.**
Stanley A. Blumberg, Gwinn Owens.   New York: G. Putnam's Sons, 1981. 307p.

This is a general account of the role of Israeli intelligence, including the Mossad, in the growth of the State of Israel and its preservation. The work follows the premise that Israel's continued existence is dependent upon the continued success of the various intelligence services in protecting the state from the hostile states on all her borders and from the Palestinian Liberation movements. The work goes back to the early Zionist intelligence agencies during the First World War, the NILI network, the illegal immigration from Europe, the Haganah, and the Mossad Aliyah Beth. Following the creation of the State of Israel in 1948 the work deals with the operations of all of the intelligence agencies in countering Arab military aggression, terrorism within Israel, and actions against Israeli targets overseas.

34 **The Iron Wall: Zionist revisionism from Jacotinsky to Shamir.**
Lennie Brenner. London: Zed Books, 1984. 221p. bibliog.
A comprehensive documented history of 'revisionism', the dominant ideological tendency in present-day Zionism. This ideology argues that no compromise is possible with the Palestinians and provides the basis for conservative Israeli policies. The work covers early Israeli movements such as the Haganah and the Stern Gang, Jewish underground activities, and special operations of the Israeli secret services. The role of the Mossad is considered, especially in relation to covert activity in partnership with South Africa dealing with the training of internal security forces and counter-intelligence.

35 **From Tel Aviv: spies and spooks.**
Jay Bushinsky. *Present Tense*, vol. 4, no. 3 (1977), p. 21-4. bibliog.
Bushinsky describes the main branches of the Israeli intelligence services, including the Mossad, and their impact on the intelligence services of the Arab states and the superpowers. In the latter case the connections between the Israeli services and the CIA are explored. He also describes the reforms instigated in Israel as a result of the intelligence débâcle at the time of the Yom Kippur war. Some successful and unsuccessful Israeli, Arab, Soviet, and United States operations are described.

36 **The untold history of Israel.**
Jacques Derogy, Hesi Carmel. New York: Grove Press, 1979. 346p. bibliog.
This work [published in France as *Histoire secrète d'Israël 1917-1977*. Orban, 1978] presents the intelligence background to many of the key events in the history of Israel from 1948, particularly in relation to the Arab–Israeli wars. There are numerous references throughout the text to Mossad and its operations.

37 **Israeli intelligence: tactics, strategy and prediction.**
Gideon Doran. *International Journal of Intelligence and Counterintelligence*, vol. 2, no. 3 (1988), p. 305-19.
An examination of the overall operations of the various branches of the Israeli intelligence services, including the Mossad. Doran deals largely with the strategy and tactics being pursued in defence of the state.

38 **Israeli intelligence: utility and cost-effectiveness in policy formation.**
Gideon Doran, Reuven Pedatzur. *International Journal of Intelligence and Counterintelligence*, vol. 3, no. 1 (1989), p. 347-61.
A study of the Israeli intelligence services whose role is to maintain the security of the country, influenced by the threat posed by its Arab neighbours. As such, the intelligence services are interwoven with the determination of military doctrine and philosophy and provide an effective deterrent to potential and actual aggression. The

Israeli Intelligence: General

intelligence service is regarded as cost-effective for the military as the lack of such an input would result in higher security costs and an increased strain on the Israeli economy. Both the structure and the function of the intelligence services are examined, together with the failure of 1973 over the Yom Kippur war, and the recommendations of the Agronat Commission – especially in relation to the Mossad. The main concentration is on Military Intelligence and the role of Aman, and the authors conclude with an examination of the channels open to the intelligence community in reporting and interpreting data for Israel's policy-makers.

39 L'Oeil de Tel-Aviv. (The eye of Tel-Aviv.)
Steve Eytan.   Paris: Editions et Publications Premières, 1970. 305p. bibliog.

This French-language work deals with the Israeli intelligence services and their operations in the capture of Adolf Eichmann, the capture of a MiG 21 fighter from Iraq, a radar system from Egypt and patrol boats from Cherbourg. The Mossad is dealt with in a specific section (p. 15-29) covering its founding, early activities, and development as the key intelligence gatherer for Israel.

40 Israel observed: an anatomy of the state.
William Frankel.   London: Thames & Hudson, 1980. 288p. bibliog.

A study of the major sources of power in Israel, including the workings of the Knesset, political parties, the electoral system, religious establishments, the legal system, the media, and the armed forces. There is little specific to the Mossad which is briefly dealt with under a section on intelligence.

41 Guards without frontiers: Israel's war against terrorism.
Samuel M. Katz.   London: Arms and Armour, 1990. 221p. map. bibliog.

This illustrated work tells the story of Israel's struggle to maintain its existence and, in particular, the constant fight against terrorism. In addition to the Israeli Defence Forces the state relies on three agencies: the Mossad which is the foreign intelligence service; Shin Beth the internal security service covering Israel and the occupied territories; and the National Police Border Guards. The book deals with the work of the three agencies in an often covert war waged throughout the world in order to protect Israel and her citizens. The three agencies are dealt with separately, with the Mossad being covered in the Introduction and between pages 21 and 67. The study is primarily concerned with the struggle against terrorism and covers the background to the rise of Palestinian terror groups, the period between 1967 and 1972, Mossad's war against Black September, and activity against the Popular Front for the Liberation of Palestine. However, in order to place this in the context of the wider scene this section of the book also deals with the origins of Mossad, its structures, the various controllers, and its other major intelligence successes and activities. The section concludes with the problems encountered by the Mossad in the 1980s, the low morale of the service, and the loss of confidence by the population within Israel after several public revelations about the agency's failures. The Mossad is also dealt with in the fifth section of the book (p. 177-202) which covers the specific operations against the terrorists Abu Jihad and Ahmed Jibril. The study concludes with a chronicle of terrorist operations and there is also an organizational chart of the structure of the Mossad.

Israeli Intelligence: General

42 Fundamental surprise: the national intelligence crisis.
Zvi Lanir. Tel Aviv: United Kibbutz Publications, 1983.

43 Hot money and the politics of debt.
R. T. Naylor. New York: Simon & Schuster, 1987. 463p. bibliog.

Naylor's comprehensive, scholarly, world-wide survey of large-scale international money-lending activities is extensively illustrated with references to institutions, personalities and activities. It includes consideration of the role of the secret services in these activities, including individual members of the Mossad. The author also discusses the lending of money by the Mossad to the Swiss banking sector.

44 Secret police: the inside story of a network of terror.
Thomas Plate, Andrea Darvi. New York: Doubleday & Co., 1981. 458p.

This work has numerous references to state security and the secret services of Israel, including the Mossad.

45 Israel undercover: secret warfare and hidden diplomacy in the Middle East.
Steve Posner. Syracuse, New York: Syracuse University Press, 1987. 350p. bibliog.

A detailed review and analysis of Israeli paramilitary, counter-intelligence operations against Palestinian guerrillas, and of secret negotiations carried out among Arab statesmen, Israeli leaders and United States officials from the late 1960s to 1987. The main focus is on Israel's use of her intelligence network, including the Mossad, to conduct military reprisals during the 1970s. The work has extensive coverage of espionage and covert action related to secret diplomacy and counter-terrorism. The Mossad is extensively covered, with particular reference to the Munich Olympic Games massacre; Brad Kirkland, a Mossad double agent; and the invasion of Lebanon in 1982. The work is based on seven years of research and extensive interviews. Some news, places, dates and other related details have been fictionalized by the author for reasons of security.

46 Every spy a prince: the complete history of Israel's intelligence community.
Dan Raviv, Yossi Melman. New York; London: Houghton Mifflin, 1991. xii, 473p. bibliog.

Published in the UK as *The imperfect spies*, this is an extremely detailed study of Israel's intelligence services, including the Mossad. The prologue to the work is a good survey of the development of the services, giving the reasons for the founding of the various services, all of which owed their origins to the struggle for the Jewish state, the problem of the diaspora in Europe, and the encouragement of illegal immigration into Palestine. The survey points to the successes enjoyed by the intelligence services and indicates that for a number of years Israel was unique in that its security services were overwhelmingly supported by the population as the army and clandestine agencies offered protection to the state and were considered second to none. This was reinforced by success in 1967, with intelligence providing the triumph

Israeli Intelligence: General

behind the Six Day war and the rescue of the hostages in 1976 at Entebbe airport. The situation had altered by the 1980s, with major changes both in public opinion and in the performance of the services. The invasion of Lebanon in 1982 was an operation that went sour when security officers were caught killing hijackers during interrogation as well as putting misplaced faith in the Christian Phalangists. This change was recognized by a retired operative at the end of the 1980s who stated, 'We have caught the CIA disease. No one seems to love the Mossad and Shin Beth anymore, and we always felt more secure and effective with the whole nation behind us'. A Mossad veteran, David Kimche, claimed that the agency was in decline as the agents were not of the same calibre as those who had joined in the 1950s. 'The main difference was the great motivation of our people. It was a matter of mission and readiness to work day and night with unlimited dedication' (*Yediot Aharonat* [Tel Aviv] vol. 2, no. 9 [16 Jan. 1987]). The work then deals with the beginnings of the intelligence agencies and the birth of the Mossad in 1951, and discusses the early work of Shiloah as director of the institute. He was not a great success in that position and was replaced in 1952 by Isser Harel who controlled the activities of Shin Beth within Israel and the Mossad abroad. One of Harel's first successes was to expose a fraud by Dan Pines, a journalist, supposedly able to help Soviet Jews through contacts in Russia, but in reality operating a scam and clearly demonstrating that the early intelligence service was in disarray, with projects being untested and consuming thousand of dollars with no return. Harel was a good administrator and he rapidly developed an intelligence empire and had more power concentrated within his hands than any other intelligence chief of the Western world had been able to achieve. The authors then go on to discuss the close relationship developed with France and the various strategic alliances including the CIA, operations in the Soviet Union, and the movement of Jews from Morocco as a co-operative venture between Israel, France and Morocco. The Mossad suffered setbacks in an operation in West Germany over the work being done by German scientists on rockets for the Egyptian government; two agents were arrested. The whole venture was seen as a crusade on the part of Harel and despite instructions from David Ben-Gurion he refused to back down and resigned on 25 March 1963 after two Mossad agents were arrested in Switzerland. The Mossad then came under the direction of Major General Meir Amit who was the first outsider to join the agency as its head, but his appointment was not popular amongst agency operatives in Europe. At the same time Amit was still operating as head of Aman and he used this position to begin a reconstruction of the organization by bringing the élite operations arm of Aman unit 131 into the Mossad. He subsequently installed his own staff, mainly from Aman, into the Mossad as supporters of Harel left or resigned, knowing that support for Harel had ruined their career prospects. The organization moved into new premises and pursued a process of modernization, including a systematic recruiting policy rather than reliance on the 'old-boy' network. The work then considers the history and development of the Mossad and its various operations, including those that failed, and the problems of trying to infiltrate and deal with the Palestine Liberation Organization. However, it is argued by the authors that Israel should not expect too much of its intelligence services as it can be only 'an excellent example of what a small nation with meagre resources can do by using them to the utmost. The community's history has demonstrated both the inescapable limitations and the maximal achievement of intelligence'.

47 **The war against terror: national policy and the security of Israel.**
    Tel Aviv: Revivin Publishing House, 1988.

Mossad: General

48 **Anatomy of a covert operation: inside Israel's secret army.**
James Adams. *TV Guide* (Radnor, PA), vol. 38, no. 11 (March 1990), p. 25-7.

An account of the trial and conviction of Mordechai Vananu who had sold details of Israel's secret nuclear weapons stockpile to the British press. Adams also considers the activities of the Mossad in general.

49 **Spies in the Promised Land: Isar Harel and the Israeli Secret Service.**
Michel Bar-Zohar. London: Davis-Poynter, 1972. 292p.

This is an excellent biography of Isser Harel who rose to become the head of all the agencies of national security from the founding of the State of Israel until his resignation in 1963. The biography deals with Harel's early life in Europe, his illegal immigration into Palestine, and his work with the Jewish underground and the Haganah. In 1948 he was made head of Shin Bet, the Israeli internal security service, becoming head of the Mossad in September 1952 following the resignation of Reuven Shiloach after only one year as its head – he had proved to be lacking in practicality, perseverance, and organizational ability. The bulk of the work is concerned with Harel's period as Head of the Mossad and director of all the security agencies, though the work is not just a consideration of the Mossad but of the intelligence services generally. However, in March 1963 Harel resigned, after a major policy disagreement with Ben-Gurion over the threat posed by German scientists working on rockets in Egypt and over the actions to be taken to neutralize the threat. The issue caused hysteria in the Israeli press though, in retrospect, the threat was minimal because of the nature of the technology (which was obsolete), and because of the paucity of raw materials available in Egypt. It was only on 1 April 1963 that Harel's name and position was disclosed to the public and the Israeli press. This is an extremely readable, detailed account which could have been improved by an index and a bibliography.

Mossad: General

50 Security or Armageddon: Israel's nuclear strategy.
Edited by Louis Rene Beres. Lexington, Massachusetts: Lexington Books, 1986. 242p.

This work deals with the Israeli government's objective of obtaining a nuclear capability for defence purposes, though the work indicates that Armageddon could be the final result if there was nuclear proliferation amongst the protagonists in the Middle East. The Mossad was one of the agencies involved in covert action around the world to acquire knowledge, materials and components, whilst at the same time providing intelligence data on moves by the Arab states to acquire a nuclear capability. It was intelligence provided by the Mossad which led to the raid on the Iraqi nuclear reactor on 7 June 1981.

51 Dirty business as usual for death or glory men.
Shyam Bhatia. *Observer* (London), no. 10562 (20 March 1944), p. 19.

Bhatia discusses the activities of the Mossad in the Arab world, particularly in relation to weapons development in the Arab states and the possibility of a nuclear threat from Iraq or Iran. The Palestinians are also regarded as a security threat by the Mossad which uses PLO officials as sources of intelligence. Adnan Yassin was an official who spied for the Mossad but was discovered, arrested, and imprisoned by the PLO.

52 The spy from Israel.
Ben Dan. London: Vallentine Mitchell, 1969. 212p.

This is an account of one of Israel's most successful secret agents, Eli Cohen, who had operated very efficiently in Syria for three years from 1962 to 1965 when he was caught by the Syrians, secretly tried, and publicly hanged. Cohen had been trained in Israel before being sent to Argentina in order to establish his identity as an Arab from South America. After arriving in Damascus Cohen penetrated circles close to the Syrian government and upper echelons of the armed forces, including the nephew of the Commander-in-Chief. He was also befriended by an official of the Ministry of Information who found him a job broadcasting on Syrian radio on behalf of the Ba'ath party. Cohen worked entirely on his own but the levels of Syrian society that he penetrated as Kamal Amin Taabes, and the quality of his intelligence, was such that Israel was able, during the Six Day war of 1967, to defeat the Syrian forces within a matter of hours and to capture the Golan Heights. A number of Syrians were also arrested and tried with Cohen, not because of any active part in espionage activities, but because they had been intimate friends of Cohen for three years and had been taken in by his performance as a South American Arab. Despite world-wide appeals for clemency for Cohen the execution was carried out on 18 May 1965. [Ben Dan is the pen-name of two Israeli journalists Ben Porat and Uri Dan.]

53 Blood libel: the inside story of General Ariel Sharon's history-making suit against *Time* magazine.
Uri Dan. New York: Simon & Schuster, 1987. 270p. bibliog.

The inside story of Sharon's unsuccessful libel case against *Time* magazine which had accused him of plotting with Sheikh Pierre Gemayel to avenge the murder of his son by raiding the Palestinian camps of Sabra and Shatilla. References to the Mossad are limited and mainly relate to their presence at interviews between Sharon and Gemayel after the death of the latter's son.

Mossad: General

54 **The Plumbatt affair.**
Elaine Davenport, Paul Eddy, Peter Gillman.   London: Deutsch, 1978.
191p.
An account of the seizure by the Israelis of a shipment of uranium ore from the *Schensbeg* in 1968.

55 **The Israeli secret services.**
Richard Deacon.   London: Hamish Hamilton, 1977. 356p. bibliog.
This study of the Mossad begins by placing it into an historical context, maintaining that its roots could be traced back to the time of Moses. Although there had been a break of centuries the organization within the new State of Israel was merely building on these earlier traditions which had been sustained by individual Jews scattered throughout the world and often subjected to persecution. However, Deacon sees the beginnings of an organized Israeli intelligence service as having taken place in the late nineteenth century, with the creation of Jewish defence units within the Workers of Zion party. In Russia it was a revolutionary party, whilst in the rest of Europe it gathered intelligence on the enemies of the Jews and offered some protection to Jewish citizens through its defence units. The period between the two world wars gave rise to Zionist activity within Palestine and the rise of various organizations such as Irgun, Haganah, and Lechi. During the Second World War there were many examples of services rendered to the allies by Jews, but without recognition, and when peace arrived without moves towards the resolution of a 'National Home' extreme measures arose within the Jewish community. The priority of many Jewish organizations, especially Irgun, was to step up immigration into Palestine, whilst the Haganah sabotaged ships used to deport Jews from Palestine. The Haganah founded the Mossad Aliyah Beth in 1937 as a secret army to carry out large-scale immigration into Palestine and the present-day Mossad grew from this organization. At the same time the Shai (Information Service) was established for intelligence gathering within Palestine, and Mossad worked effectively using information supplied by Shai who were represented in all aspects of the mandatory administration and efficiently monitored developments within the Arab community. The creation of the State of Israel in 1948 created the need for a foreign intelligence-gathering network and the Mossad was ideally placed to fulfil this role. The first few chapters of Deacon's work are excellent at discussing these various developments in Palestine and Europe together with the inter-relationship between the various Jewish Zionist organizations. After independence the Israeli state found that it had an espionage war on two fronts from the Arabs and Russia, whilst a third enemy was represented by the Nazis who had fled to many parts of the world, particularly South America, the USSR, and Spain. The first real controller of the modern-day Mossad was Isser Harel, who was not only adept at gathering intelligence but also in its interpretation, and he developed the links already established in Europe through the underground networks. The book then goes on to discuss various notable Mossad operations such as the work of Eli Cohen in Syria, the capture of Adolf Eichmann, the work of Wolfgang Lotz the 'Champagne Spy' in Egypt, successes in the Six Day war, the obtaining of blueprints of the Mirage jet fighter, and the liberation of Israeli gunboats from Cherbourg in 1969, despite the French arms embargo which had been imposed in 1968. Further chapters deal with the raid on Entebbe, actions against Palestinian guerrilla fighters, including the failed operation at Lillehammer, and the lessons learned from the Yom Kippur war which was not an intelligence failure but rather an administrative failure within the Israeli government. Deacon also deals with the links, often unofficial, between the Israelis and other Western secret services.

Mossad: General

56 Decline of the superspies.
Time Magazine (23 March 1987), p. 32.
At one time the Mossad was ranked as a world-class service with the capture of Adolf Eichmann being one of its acknowledged successes. The networks developed by the Mossad and Shin Bet were so effective that they were relied upon by the CIA for information and analysis, and their effectiveness was recognized even when the objectives were debatable. The author of this article concludes, however, that the apparatus seemed to be in decline with the leaking of the nuclear weapons programme by Mordechai Vananu and his subsequent kidnapping by the Mossad which strained relations with Britain and Italy. Shin Bet was also under a cloud because of its involvement in the murder of two Arab hijackers.

57 The Mossad: Israel's secret intelligence service.
Dennis Eisenberg, Uri Dan, Eli Landau. New York: Signet, 1978. 264p.
A recounting of some of the activities of the Mossad, though in specific cases some names and biographical details of active agents were changed to protect their identities. The primary objective of the Mossad when it was established by Ben-Gurion was to gather and analyse information abroad, in any area that might be of interest to Israel. However, specific assignments were also allocated to the Mossad allowing it to perform any unusual operations which fell outside other arms of government, either civilian or military. The work covers the following main areas: the rise to power of Isser Harel as head of the Mossad, and subsequently, the head of all of Israel's intelligence services; the Eichmann kidnapping; the strange case of Jossele, a Jewish boy kidnapped from his secular parents by Orthodox grandparents; the Six Day war; struggles against arms embargoes; and detection of anti-Israeli spies.

58 Spook Kook.
Steve Emerson. *New Republic*, vol. 203, no. 21 (Nov. 1990), p. 13-14.
An examination of Ostrovsky's *By way of deception* (see item no. 65) and, in particular, his claim that the Mossad had advance intelligence of the Beirut bombing of the US marine barracks which was not passed on to the United States. The article criticizes Ostrovsky's credentials and his claims.

59 Painter, poet, soldier, spy.
Milton Esterow. *ARTnews*, vol. 94, no. 3 (1995), p. 114-19.
A consideration of the life and work of Peter Malkin, a former Mossad agent, who was largely responsible for engineering the capture of Adolf Eichmann in Argentina. However, he is also a talented painter who has exhibited widely.

60 Temporary ban on Mossad book is overturned in US and Canada.
Howard Field. *Publishers Weekly*, vol. 237 (28 Sept. 1990), p. 10-11.
This is an account of the court hearing which overturned a temporary injunction secured by the Israeli government to prevent the publication of Victor Ostrovsky's *By way of deception* (see item no. 65). The injunction had been granted on the grounds that publication could 'endanger the lives of various people in the employ of the State of Israel' but the New York State Supreme Court overturned the injunction on the

Mossad: General

grounds that the claim by the Israeli government had not been sufficiently supported. This article is representative of a number of similar articles in *Macleans*, *Time*, and *Newsweek*.

61 **Israel's elite intelligence corps: exploits of the accomplished and respected 'Eye of David'.**
Erich Follath. *World Press Review*, vol. 27 (May 1980), p. 29-31.
An overview of activities of the Mossad. Adapted from an article which appeared in *Stern*, it deals with Operation Plumbatt in 1968 when piracy was used to acquire uranium for Israel's nuclear programme; the attack on shipments of nuclear components held in France in 1979 for despatch to Iraq; and other activities such as those of Wolfgang Lotz in Egypt and the kidnapping of Eichmann. Follath also considers the position of the Mossad within Israel, its methods of recruitment and training, and links with other agencies such as the CIA and Iran's SAVAK.

62 **A man of mystery sells a chilling story and then vanishes.**
Ken Gross. *People Weekly*, vol. 26 (17 Nov. 1986), p. 61-3.
Israel was shaken when Mordechai Vananu sold the secrets of Israel's nuclear stockpile to the *Sunday Times* (London) for £50,000. Vananu was a technician at Israel's nuclear research site at Dimna who was sacked from his post and he left with a grudge and rolls of films and notes designed to expose the secret stockpile. The evidence showed that Israel had manufactured between 100 and 200 nuclear weapons at Dimna, with the film providing a blueprint of its operations. Vananu disappeared from his London hotel before collecting his fee and hints from Israel indicated that he had been kidnapped by the Mossad.

63 **As Israel tries to smother his book a former Mossad spy spills some dark secrets of that shadowy service.**
Ken Gross. *People Weekly*, vol. 34, no. 13 (Oct. 1990), p. 105-6.
This interview with Victor Ostrovsky over his book *By way of deception* (q.v.) includes the legal efforts by Israel to have the book banned in Canada and the United States. Although acknowledged as a member of the Mossad from 1984 to 1986 Israel insisted that he was only a junior clerk, had left-wing tendencies, and was eager for money. The interview also covers some of the revelations in the book, including the Beirut bombing of the US Marine barracks of which he asserts the Mossad had advance intelligence which it did not share with the United States. Ostrovsky left the Mossad in 1986 under unclear circumstances with the interviewee claiming that he had made enemies of important officials, whilst Israel maintains it was on the grounds of incompetence.

64 **One-man Mossad: Reuven Shiloah father of Israeli intelligence.**
Eshed Hagai. Tel Aviv: Edanim Yediot Aharonat, 1988. (In Hebrew).

65 **By way of deception: an insider's devastating exposé of the Mossad.**
Claire Hoy, Victor Ostrovsky. London: Bloomsbury Publishing; New York: St Martin's Press, 1990. 371p.
This is an important, but controversial, book which has been branded as a fraud by the Israeli authorities. Although Israel admits that Ostrovsky was a member of the Mossad

Mossad: General

from 1984 to 1986 they contend that he was a very junior clerk with left-wing tendencies and an ambition to make money. This is contested by the author who claims that he was recruited to be a case officer for the Mossad after having turned down earlier requests to join the organization's assassination unit. Ostrovsky was from Zionist roots and had Israeli and Canadian citizenship but was brought up by grandparents when his parents divorced and moved back to North America. At the age of eighteen he became an officer in the Israeli army and was in and out of military service for the next eighteen years before joining the Mossad. Although the book discusses many of the major Mossad projects and triumphs and its overall operations, the main impact was made by Ostrovsky's disclosures which alleged both orgies between leaders and young secretaries, and also the slaughter of PLO suspects. The most serious allegation levied by the author is that Israeli agents knew in advance specific details of the attack on the Beirut barracks of American marines in 1983 whilst only vague warnings were given to the United States. The reasons for Ostrovsky leaving the Mossad are unclear and equally controversial; the author claims that it was due to his making enemies of high-ranking officials by his persistent questioning of dubious activities and objectives, whilst a Mossad source maintained that he was dismissed for bumbling an assignment. In addition to the legal manoeuvres Ostrosky also maintained that he had been visited and threatened by Mossad agents in Ottawa and that he was afraid of assassination. He maintained that the book had to be written in support of his earlier Zionist ideals and principles which experiences within the Mossad had devalued. A large part of the book is concerned with Ostrovsky's training programme and the various programmes followed by the recruits before becoming active agents.

66   **Israel blocks embarrassing book briefly in U.S., Canada.**
     News Media and the Law, vol. 14, no. 4 (Fall 1990), p. 5-6.
An account of the legal background to Israel's attempt to block publication of Ostrovsky's *By way of deception* (q.v.) in Canada and the United States. It covers the defence issues in relation to freedom of the press and freedom of speech.

67   **Vengeance: the true story of a counter-terrorism mission.**
     George Jonas.   London: Collins, 1984. 444p. bibliog.
Published in New York by Simon & Schuster as *Vengeance: the true story of an Israeli anti-terrorist team,* this is a case-study of the Mossad team sent to avenge the massacre of Israeli athletes at the Munich Olympics in 1972. The Israeli Prime Minister, Golda Meir, decided that a team of agents should be trained to track down and kill those members of the higher echelons of the Palestine Liberation Organization responsible for the Munich massacre and other atrocities. The operation is seen through the eyes of the team leader Avner who was extensively interviewed by the author in clandestine meetings in North America. Jonas followed that with extensive enquiries in the Middle East and Europe, though some details were altered to protect his sources. The massacre at Munich was carried out in September 1972 by eight Black September terrorists, the Fedayeen, and initially two Israelis were killed and nine held captive. The demand was for the release of Palestinian prisoners in Israel but negotiations were a failure, and an attempted rescue before the hostages could be flown to Cairo was an even more tragic failure as the nine hostages were murdered and only three of the Fedayeen survived. The incident caused shock throughout the world and the Israeli government determined that revenge had to be exacted through the Mossad. The team leader Avner, aged 22, was recruited by Israeli intelligence and the work deals with his early training, his work as a sky marshal with El Al and his

surveillance activities in Europe. However, at age 26 he was taken from relative obscurity to become leader of a team set up to take retribution for the Munich massacre, an operation which took two years in the planning and training of the operatives. The unit was charged with establishing a base in Europe, to have no operational links with Israel, and provided with unlimited funds for arms and the procuring of information. The book traces the development of the mission with the tracking of the targets, the executions, and the loss of three of the team members. The account also shows how the team set about fulfilling their objective with ruthless efficiency, leading to an adoption of the same tactics as their targets and illustrating the paradox of the operation. Avner became disillusioned with the objectives of the operation, and following the loss of the third member of the team in Frankfurt in January 1975, the operation was closed down over a period of three months. In April 1975 Avner went to New York, before returning to Israel for debriefing and an investigation into the operation and the unauthorized actions of the team, but his disenchantment grew and in May 1975 he returned to New York with the intention of never returning to Israel. The Mossad pressurized him to return and removed funds from the clandestine bank account in Israel but Avner remained in America, changed his name, and severed all links with the world of espionage. The author ends his book with a personal assessment of Avner resulting from opinions formed during the interviews, and Jonas concludes that the motive for recounting the experiences was that Avner needed to relive them. On the subject of the mission Jonas concludes that Avner has no second thoughts or regrets, remains convinced of the rightness of the mission – though not of its usefulness – and, despite feeling wronged by the Mossad, his overall patriotism as an Israeli was undiminished.

68   **Tales of the Mossad.**
Craig S. Karpel.   *Penthouse* (US), vol. 11 (Jan. 1980), p. 68-72; vol. 11 (May 1980), p. 128-33.

69   **Alter ego on the loose.**
Mark Lawson.   *Independent* (London) (13 March 1993), p. 28-32.
An interview with Philip Roth in the magazine section about his novel *Operation Shylock* in which the main character is a Mossad agent called Philip Roth. The author maintains that this is autobiographical set in a fictional background.

70   **The Zionist connection: what price peace?**
Alfred M. Lilienthal.   New York: Dodd, Mead & Co., 1978. 872p.
A background study of the forces that have shaped the Middle East in relation to Israel and her neighbours. Detailed examination is given to the Zionist infiltration of the United States government and media which, the author contends, has resulted in United States foreign policy having been subordinated to a domestic quest for votes. Mossad operations which are discussed include the acquisition of 200 tons of natural uranium in 1968; the April 1973 raid on Lebanon to assassinate three Palestine Liberation Organization leaders Kamal Nasser, Mohammed Yusuf Najjo and Kamel Adwan; and the assassination in Norway of Palestinian guerrillas in 1974.

Mossad: General

71 **The Champagne Spy: Israel's master spy tells his story.**
Wolfgang Lotz.   London: Vallentine Mitchell, 1972. 240p. map.

This is an illustrated account by Lotz of his period of nearly five years in Egypt. From 1961 he operated as a Mossad agent and lived a life of extravagance in high society. He posed, with his wife, as a wealthy German horse-breeder and mixed with the higher echelons of Egyptian society, numbering senior army officers, cabinet ministers, and senior intelligence officers amongst his friends. In addition Cairo's German colony, convinced that he was an ex-SS officer in hiding, welcomed the couple into their ranks. Lotz was a German Jew with dual citizenship who had become a member of the Haganah in 1937 (when he was aged 16). He joined the British army at the outbreak of war and rejoined the Haganah after the war whilst working at the Haifa Oil Refineries. Following a period in the Israeli army from 1948, Lotz was recruited and trained by the Mossad, then went to Germany for a year to build a cover story before leaving for Egypt. Lotz was instrumental in providing a great deal of intelligence to the Mossad about the Egyptian forces and defences, but his most significant success was the uncovering of the details of the Egyptian rocket programme being developed by German scientists. He was arrested in 1965 and sentenced to life imprisonment; his wife received three years for aiding and abetting. The work concludes with an account of his period in prison and his contact with another Mossad agent Victor Levy, a casualty of the Lavon affair, also serving a life sentence. Lotz's period in prison was ended by the Six Day war when he was released, together with his wife, on medical grounds, but in reality Israel had made the repatriation of some 5,000 Egyptian prisoners, including nine generals, conditional upon their release.

72 **Inside the Mossad: Israel tries to ban a book embarrassing to its top-secret agency.**
Tom Masland.   *Newsweek,* vol. 116 (24 Sept. 1990), p. 33-4.

An account of the attempt by Israel to stop the publication of Victor Ostrovsky's *By way of deception* (see item no. 65) in Canada and the United States.

73 **Eli Cohen: le combattant de Damas.** (Eli Cohen: the fighter from Damascus.)
Jacques Mercier.   Paris: Laffont, 1982. 319p.

A French-language biography of Eli Cohen who was an agent for the Mossad operating in Syria. Cohen was a successful operative who gained the trust of the Ba'ath hierarchy to such an extent that he joined in the deliberations of its executive community and was able to supply Israel with much strategic information. Cohen was arrested, tried and sentenced to death on 18 May 1965.

74 **Dossier secret sur Israël: le terrorisme.** (Secret dossier on Israel: terrorism.)
Vincent Moniteil.   Paris: Guy Authier, 1978. 414p. bibliog.

An illustrated French-language work which takes the standpoint that Israel is a terrorist state using the Holocaust as an alibi. It details the horrors of terrorist activities on the part of both Arabs and Israelis and has a section entitled 'Les Crimes du Mossad en Europe', detailing various operations carried out by Mossad operatives.

Mossad: General

75 **Mossad: Israel's most secret service.**
Ronald Payne. London; New York: Bantam Press, 1990. 233p. bibliog.

The Mossad, more properly the Institute for Intelligence and Special Services, is an institute with an academic and scientific basis backed up with a special services operation. At the outset Payne maintains that the operatives of Israeli intelligence are more dedicated than their colleagues in other organizations on account of the constant threats beyond their borders and the long shadow of the Holocaust when Jews appeared to go to death 'like lambs to a slaughter'. The reputation of the Mossad is also discussed, with its description as the best intelligence service in the world being based on a reputation for devotion and efficiency. Isser Harel, the second head of Mossad, said the following in relation to this reputation: 'They should stop spinning legends around Mossad. I think that we just work harder and collect more information than the others. No other country in the world has such urgent need for an efficient secret service. Israel is surrounded by enemies. We have no diplomatic relations with these nations whose agents clobber us as terrorists. For us it is a question of survival.' However, this reputation was sullied once the Mossad became involved with the Palestinians and terrorism, and the invasion of the Lebanon; the essential underground war became a corrupting operation and admiration for the Mossad turned to suspicion about its clandestine operations. In the early days the existence of the Mossad was not officially recognized and this was not surprising as the organization grew out of the clandestine operations to organize Jewish immigration into Palestine. This concept was readily accepted in the new State of Israel as many of its political leaders had been members of the intelligence community: Chaim Herzog had been in military intelligence; Yitzhat Shamir was a Mossad field man in Europe; and David Kimche, a senior foreign ministry civil servant, had been a deputy director of Mossad. Thus the secret beginnings and its traditions established the pattern which was maintained and became a normal pattern after independence. The work of Israeli intelligence in its early days was characterized by a disaster in Egypt between 1954 and 1955 when Operation Suzanna went badly wrong. Eleven operatives in Egypt were arrested, two of whom were executed, Max Bennett killed himself in prison by opening his veins with a rusty nail, and the others received long prison sentences. The situation was not helped by the failure of Mossad and Aman, the military intelligence, to provide detailed intelligence about relations between Egypt and the Soviet Union, and the arms deal with Czechoslovakia. However, Mossad and Aman had been successful in keeping secret the contacts between Israel, Britain and France in the summer and autumn of 1956 over the preparations for the Suez war. It was the failure of the Suez adventure that encouraged the Mossad to direct its attentions elsewhere as a means of restoring domestic self-confidence and to remind the world of Jewish suffering by renewing efforts to bring ex-Nazis to justice. This led to the operation to capture Adolf Eichmann who was kidnapped from Argentina in 1960, tried and executed. The operation had taken two years of planning under the direction of Isser Harel and did much for the world-wide reputation of the Mossad as the boldest intelligence service in the world. Payne also considers the activities of Wolfgang Lotz in Egypt, and the adoption by Mossad of the new technology to provide intelligence, which was a main factor in the military triumph of the Six Day war. However, the ensuing years saw the rise of Palestinian guerrilla and terrorist activity which resulted in Mossad resources being fully deployed in trying to combat this subversive workforce and extra staff were recruited to the service. A large section of the work deals with these activities and the counter-terrorism role of the Mossad and other Israeli intelligence agencies, as well as the infrastructure problems created by the Yom Kippur war when intelligence was obtained and wasted. This section concludes with the question of Israeli involvement in Lebanon, secret contact with the Christians, and a mistaken belief that an alliance with Phalange would secure its borders. This was an error of judgement and the Mossad failed to use its intelligence information to prevent the resultant political disaster. Sections five and six of the work deal with Israel's relations with her allies, such as President Sadat, and the close working relationship with the CIA. Section six also deals with Israeli actions against Iraq's nuclear capability, the Jonathan Jay Pollard affair in the United States in 1984 when he was accused of spying for Israel, and Mossad operations in Africa. The work concludes with a study of what had gone wrong with Israeli intelligence and the Mossad; the problem is seen as being intertwined with the misfortunes of Israel itself. The removal of censorship also led to criticism of the Mossad which no longer enjoyed its status as a miracle-worker. However, any present-day successes still remain hidden by the law of secrecy whilst its blunders are exposed to public scrutiny. The writer is a professional journalist who has produced a detailed study of the Mossad and its place in Israel's history which is extremely informative yet readable.

76 **Israeli intelligence over the years.**
    Victor Perry.   *Midstream*, vol. 34 (May 1988), p. 34-6.

A brief survey of the Israeli intelligence service, the Mossad, highlighted by the Pollard case in the United States, which shook Israel's intelligence services but did not damage co-operation between the two states. For both states the exchange of information is considered too valuable for even severe shocks such as the Pollard case to damage the relationship. Further examples of operations are outlined such as Operation Suzanna in Egypt, the rescue of Jews from Morocco, operations against Palestinian guerrillas, and operations in the Lebanon in 1982. Perry also mentions the memorial to the fallen of Israel's intelligence over the years from 1947.

77 **The boats of Cherbourg.**
    Abraham Rabinovich, Steve Posner.   New York: Henry Holt & Co., 1988.

An account of the raid by Mossad agents to retrieve patrol boats from Cherbourg which had been part of an arms deal with France but the sale had been blocked at the last moment.

78 **Israel: the man from the Mossad.**
    Meir Ronnan.   *ARTnews*, vol. 91, no. 5 (May 1992), p. 141.

Covers the drawing made by Peter Malkin during his trip to Argentina as part of the Mossad team involved in the Eichmann operation.

79 **A spy in Canaan: my life as a Jewish-American businessman spying for Israel in Arab lands.**
    Howard H. Schack.   New York: Birch Lane, 1993. 256p.

The author volunteered to spy for the Mossad after the Yom Kippur war when Israel's vulnerability was exposed. He worked for the Mossad from the mid-1970s to the late 1980s. Using the name Howard Mackenzie, he operated in a number of Arab countries as a non-ideological businessman. His activities included provision of intelligence which contributed to the success of the Entebbe operation, and information on Iraq's Ossirah plant which led to the 1981 Israeli bombing.

Mossad: General

80 **The spymasters of Israel.**
Stewart Steven. London; New York: Macmillan, 1980. 329p. bibliog.

This study is based on extensive interviews with Mossad agents from around the world and with officials in Tel Aviv. Steven provides an account of the birth, growth, and operations of the Mossad, covering the blunders as well as the successes. Aspects of internal security or counter-intelligence are only briefly touched upon as the work concentrates on the overseas operations in the area of political, civilian, and military intelligence. He also discusses the internal struggle for supremacy between the Mossad and military intelligence which has not been resolved. The work stresses the significance of the intelligence services to both Arabs and Israelis in the Middle East as it has, in effect, been a constant struggle for survival. Both sides have been on a continuous war footing since 1948 and the Israeli view has been that 'We are good at our task because the alternative is too horrifying to contemplate'. Considerable detail is provided on the birth of the Mossad from its first six months of existence, when tragic mistakes were made, to its gradual evolution into an efficient and effective intelligence force. The kidnap and successful prosecution of Adolf Eichmann is considered to have thrust Israeli intelligence on to the world stage and led to the State of Israel being accorded more respect by both her friends and her enemies. The author concludes that Israel is a society inclined to hysteria – victories are greeted with enormous jubilation and defeats with national gloom – and that the intelligence services have been influenced by this atmosphere.

81 **Averting Armageddon: the Pope, diplomacy and the pursuit of peace.**
Gordon Thomas, Max Morgan-Wilts. New York: Doubleday & Co., 1984. 322p. bibliog.

An investigative journalism report on the Vatican Secretariat of State, the Pope, and their role in international affairs. The work has numerous incidental references to the Mossad.

82 **The Mossad's might: an Israeli agent comes in from the cold.**
David Todd. *Maclean's*, vol. 103, no. 39 (24 Sept. 1990), p. 60-1.

An account of the attempt made by Israel to prevent publication of *By way of deception* (q.v.) which was written by a former agent, Victor Ostrovsky, to expose the inner workings of the Mossad. Todd deals with the litigation in Canada and the United States through which Israel hoped to prevent publication on the grounds that it would endanger the lives of Mossad agents. Ostrovsky also maintained that he had been visited in Canada by Mossad agents trying to persuade him to withdraw the manuscript, together with vague warnings as to the dangers that could follow.

83 **Nuclear arms and the missing man.**
James M. Wall. *The Christian Century*, vol. 103 (19 Nov. 1986), p. 1019-20.

An account of the sale by Mordechai Vananu of secrets of Israel's stockpile of nuclear weapons to the British press and his alleged subsequent kidnapping by the Mossad.

Mossad: General

84   **The long arm of the Mossad: a rabbi's son spills some Israeli nuclear secrets.**
Russell Watson.   *Newsweek*, vol. 108 (10 Nov. 1986), p. 39-40.

An account of the affair of Mordechai Vananu who had been a technician in the Israeli nuclear research programme at Dimna and who sold details of Israel's nuclear programme to the British press. He fled Israel but was located by the Mossad, kidnapped, and tried and sentenced in Israel.

Military Intelligence

85   **Soldier spies: Israeli military intelligence.**
    Samuel M. Katz.   Novato, California: Presidio Press, 1992. 389p.
    bibliog.
This book is primarily a study of the intelligence-gathering arm of the Israeli Defence Forces, the Aman, which has been charged with the responsibility for collecting, analysing, and implementing all military intelligence. However, the work has numerous references throughout the text to the Mossad, providing a survey of its history and activities and also dealing with its relationship with Aman, particularly in the field of special operations. This was significant during the period when Isser Harel was head of both organizations. A section of specific relevance is Chapter 9, 'The super spies', which deals, amongst other topics, with Mossad activities in Egypt to counter their programme of missile development, and with the activities of Eli Cohen in Damascus prior to the Six Day war. This is an extremely valuable text on the background to the two agencies and is based on official histories, war records, declassified documents, and interviews with serving and former intelligence officers.

86   **The walls of Israel.**
    Jean Larteguy.   New York: M. Evans & Co., 1969. (First published in French. Paris: Editions et Publications Premières, 1968).
This study of the Israeli armed forces, regarded by the author as 'The walls of Israel', is based on interviews with members of the armed forces and participation in operations as an observer. There is a chapter entitled 'The intelligence services' (p. 80-97) which is primarily concerned with the Mossad, and with the case of Eli Cohen who was executed as a Mossad agent in Damascus in 1965.

87   **The Israeli army.**
    Edward Luttwak, Dan Horowitz.   London: Allen Lane, 1975. 461p.
    maps.
This work is primarily an illustrated account of the development of the Israeli army from 1948 to the end of the Yom Kippur war in 1973. However, the work does

Military Intelligence

examine the ill-conceived Lavin affair in Egypt, the successful Mossad operation encouraging an Iraqi pilot to defect with his MiG 21, and the relationship between the Mossad and the Israeli military intelligence.

88 Wars of the Jews: a military history from Biblical to modern times.
Monroe Rosenthal, Isaac Mozeson.   New York: Hippocrene Books, 1990. 297p. map. bibliog.

The authors examine militancy as an integral element of Jewish culture and show that the tenacity of the Jews can be attributed to their innovative military and political tactics. The Mossad is briefly mentioned in the section entitled 'Jewish warriors of modern era' (p. 227-61) which deals with the precursors of the Mossad, NILI, an acronym of a verse from the Bible which translates as 'The glory of Israel shall not lie dormant'. The Aaronsohn family were members of NILI and provided important intelligence information to Britain during the First World War.

89 Military deception, strategic surprise and conventional deterrence: a political analysis of Egypt and Israel, 1971-73.
Janice G. Stein. In: *Military deception and strategic surprise.* Edited by John Gosch, Amos Perlmutter.   London: Cass, 1982, p. 94-121.

An analysis of Egypt's plans to mount a surprise military attack on Israel which was postponed three times between 1971 and 1973 before being launched as a simultaneous attack with Syria on 6 October 1973, with deception being an integral part of the strategic plan. The Israeli perceptions were largely controlled by Military Intelligence who did not foresee any attack, though the Mossad were expressing scepticism at the analysis of the data being presented by Military Intelligence who felt that the deterrent factor still held sway.

Palestine: Illegal Immigration

90 **Flight and rescue.**
Yehuda Bauer.   New York: Random House, 1978. 369p. maps. bibliog.
An account of the organized escape of the Jewish survivors of Eastern Europe between 1944 and 1948. The movement established to organize the escape was called Brichah, which is Hebrew for 'flight'. The work deals with the transit centres and the role of the Mossad in the illegal immigration through consideration of the work of Ehad Avriel in Yugoslavia to secure support to use it as a transit country. This was favourably received by Tito as he saw the unrest in Palestine as part of an imperialist struggle against Britain. Similar activity took place in Czechoslovakia, with the Brichah being influenced by the Palestinian representatives of the Mossad, and the movement then spread through Central and Eastern Europe. At that time the Mossad was under Shaul Avigir, a member of Mapai, the moderate Labour party; he was determined that the organization should be responsible for all underground activities in Europe. The study is based on material in the Israeli State and Central Zionist archives, and privately held records.

91 **Years of wrath, days of glory.**
Yitshaq Ben-Ami.   New York: Speller & Sons, 1982. 601p. bibliog.
Memoirs of Irgun, covering primarily the 1930s and 1940s and centred upon the Jewish underground, illegal immigration into Palestine, and arms smuggling. The Mossad emerged from these operations and the underground and smuggling infrastructure.

92 **The secret army.**
David J. Bercuson.   New York: Stein & Day, 1984. 278p.
The story of the foreign volunteers who fought for the establishment of the Jewish state in 1948. The work includes references to the growth of the Mossad.

Palestine: Illegal Immigration

93 Cairo to Damascus.
John Roy Carlson. New York: Knopf, 1951. 491p. bibliog.

Carlson surveys Arab and German Nazi activity in the Middle East during the late 1930s and early 1940s and Dashnaq terrorism. The work is largely based upon undercover journalism into Arab nationalist elements covering nationalist movements in Cairo and Damascus. The latter part of the book deals with Arab guerrilla warfare against Israel, gun-running by the Jewish underground, acts of sabotage on both sides, and the Grand Mufti of Jerusalem's pro-Palestinian role. Carlson also considers Jewish organizations such as the Haganah and Palmach from which the Israeli secret services evolved, and the serious of assassinations perpetrated by both sides.

94 Shai: the exploits of Hagana intelligence.
Efraim Dekel. London; New York: Thomas Yoseloff, 1959. 369p.

The Haganah was set up to wage war against the British Mandatory authority, to secure Jewish immigration into Palestine, and to ensure the implementation of the Balfour Declaration and the creation of an independent Jewish state. The Shai was the intelligence service of the underground movement and this is an account of its development and activities concluding with the creation of the state of Israel. The Shai worked very closely with the Mossad Aliyah Beth to further the immigration of uncertified Jews into Palestine. The Mossad was responsible for the organization of the movement of migrants to Palestine, working closely with the Haganah, and it was the Shai which assisted them once in Palestine to avoid arrest and deportation. The Mossad, at that time, worked as an independent body, but under a framework laid down by Jewish institutions such as the Jewish Agency for Palestine, and liaised closely with the Haganah. The Mossad had thousands of workers within the organization, operating in scores of countries, and had branches in hundreds of ports, yet it still managed to maintain a degree of secrecy thanks to the dedication of its operatives. The agency developed its own intelligence network and obtained data from a variety of government offices and British official sources, whilst the Shai obtained intelligence on activities against illegal immigration taken by the British authorities. This structure and expertise was to be used for the creation of the Mossad as a foreign intelligence service for the newly independent state.

95 Second exodus: the full story of Jewish illegal immigration to Palestine, 1945-1948.
Ze'ev Venia Hadari. London: Vallentine Mitchell, 1991. 309p.

Hadari gives an account of illegal immigration into Palestine from the 1930s to the creation of the State of Israel in 1948. The work is divided into three periods of immigration, beginning with the period before the Second World War and the impact of the disaster that was to befall the Jews in Europe. The second period is that of the war years themselves, and the third the period after the war when the survivors of the Holocaust were desperate to get out to the only place where they felt welcome and safe. Further pressures came from Jewish populations in areas liberated by the Soviet Union who felt threatened by anti-Semitic policies and a continuation of the programmes of the revolution. The author was involved in the illegal immigration from Europe as part of the Jewish underground operating under the code name Venia. The Mossad's real origins date back to this time with the establishment of the Mossad Aliyah Beth. Chapters four to six (p. 20-55) deal with the early leaders of the organization and their influence and role; the sources of the Mossad's authority, which at that time was derived from the Jewish Agency for Palestine; and their aims and methods, particularly in the use of shipping to smuggle the immigrants into Palestine. The second main section of the work (p. 97-226) covers Mossad activities throughout the world, concentrating on immigration from the Balkans, the use of large ships for smuggling the refugees which presented a major logistical problem for the organization, immigration from Italy and France, and conflicts between Britain and France over immigration into Palestine. It was from this organization, with its networks of contacts and sympathizers throughout Europe, that the present-day Mossad was developed. An understanding of these illegal immigrations from Europe and the organization behind them forms a crucial background to this branch of Israeli intelligence.

96 **The secret roads: the illegal migration of a people.**
Jon Kimche, David Kimche.   London: Secker & Warburg, 1954. 233p.

A study of the illegal migration of Jews from Europe during and after the Second World War. The organization of the underground Jewish migration by Zionist activists proved to be the origins of the Mossad. Of particular relevance is Chapter XIII, 'The Mossad machine – confounding military intelligence' (p. 164-74). This deals with the development of the Mossad organization in Paris from late 1945, designed to organize the illegal transfer of Jews to Palestine. By 1946 it had emerged as a widely ramified and highly organized movement supported by exceptionally large financial contributions from Zionist sources. This section also discusses the sources of Mossad's funding, and discusses its structure, organization, and recruitment procedures.

97 **The Third Reich and the Palestine question.**
Francis R. Nicosia.   Austin, Texas: University of Texas Press, 1985. 319p. bibliog.

Nicosia gives an extremely detailed account of the policy of the Third Reich towards Palestine and the policy being pursued towards the Jews in the Third Reich. At one stage illegal emigration to Palestine was sanctioned by the German authorities, though without official participation, and Reinhard Heydrich of the Sicherheitsdienst (SD) was an advocate of the promotion of illegal emigration of Jews through transit countries. The work covers the foundation of the Mossad Aliyah Beth in 1937 with a base in Paris; the nucleus of the operation was then three men, Yehuda Ragin, Ze'ev Shind and Zvi Yehieli, but it soon grew to have agents throughout Europe and the Middle East. Mossad agents were instructed to set up a working relationship with the Gestapo and the SD and the two Nazi organizations were receptive to the Mossad's initiatives for co-operation. Amongst examples cited are agreements for the emigration of Austrian Jews, and Jews from Berlin and Prague, but the operations were abandoned with the outbreak of war in September 1939. However, between 1938 and 1948 the Mossad were still responsible for the illegal emigration of 100,000 Jews from Europe.

98 **The rescue of European Jewry and illegal immigration to Palestine in 1940 – prospects and reality: Berthold Storfer and the Mossad Lie' Aliyah Bet.**
Dalia Ofer.   *Modern Judaism*, vol. 4, no. 2 (1984), p. 159-81.

This article examines the emigration from Europe of Jews between 1933 and 1940 and their illegal immigration into Palestine. The author compares the operations conducted independently by a businessman, Berthold Storfer, and by the Mossad.

Palestine: Illegal Immigration

99   **On the second immigration from Romania and its way.**
Ephraim Ophir.   *Yalkut Moreshet* (Israel), vol. 31, no. 1 (1981), p. 39-74.

Ophir has studied the second wave of illegal immigration from Romania into Palestine between 1938 and 1941. The Jewish emigration was supported by the Romanian government for its own political reasons but the country also became a transit country for other European Jews. The Revisionist Movement smuggled about 10,000 Jews from Romania to Palestine whilst the Mossad, an independent operation, organized the emigration of about 4,350 people. Additional numbers of Jews independently organized their own routes out of Romania.

100   **The Jews were expendable: Free World diplomacy and the Holocaust.**
Mority Noam Pakower.   Urbana, Illinois: University of Illinois Press, 1983. 429p.

A scholarly treatment of the Free World's failure to respond to the Holocaust of 1938 and during the Second World War. This is a well-resourced study with detailed annotations and numerous references to the Jewish underground and the origins of the Mossad.

101   **The four-front war: from the Holocaust to the Promised Land.**
William R. Perl.   New York: Crown, 1979. 376p.

A study of rescue operations between 1937 and 1944 to bring European Jews to Palestine. The underground route was organized by Jewish activists and the accompanying intelligence network proved to be the origin of the Mossad.

102   **A history of the Israeli army (1974 to the present).**
Ze'ev Schiff.   New York: Macmillan, 1985. 274p.

An authoritative historical survey of the Israeli armed forces from their Zionist settler origins to the present day, with an emphasis on the Israeli army. The work also covers the activities of Jewish underground organizations, intelligence and security services, and the role of special forces. Although primarily concerned with military intelligence, the role of the Mossad in the early immigrations operations and subsequent activities is also considered.

103   **Underground to Palestine and reflections thirty years later.**
I. F. Stone.   London: Hutchinson, 1979. 260p.

This work was written in 1946 when the survivors of the Holocaust were trying to make their way to Palestine in the face of a blockade by the British Mandatory administration. The author, a journalist, accompanied Jewish refugees on their dangerous journey from the refugee camps of Eastern Europe across the continent for passage by boat to Palestine and clandestine landings on the coast. This work is not a serious academic study, but a highly personal account of a tragedy crucial to the development of the State of Israel. It is included because the underground network of agents in Europe formed the basis of the Mossad following its founding in 1952.

Palestine: Illegal Immigration

104 **Cross roads to Israel: Palestine from Balfour to Bevin.**
Christopher Sykes. London: Collins, 1965. 479p.

An illustrated history of Palestine and the Zionist movement under the British Mandate, based on the papers of Sir Mark Sykes, and on the archives of both the Military Administration of Palestine and the Civil Mandatory Government. The last two sources are now part of the Israeli State Archives. References to the Mossad are limited to its work in organizing illegal immigration into Palestine.

105 **The secret alliance: the extraordinary story of the rescue of the Jews since World War II.**
Tad Szulc. London: Pan Books, 1992. 328p. map. bibliog.

Szulc tells the story of the vital but secret role played by American Jews in the rescue of approximately two million Jews in Eastern Europe, North Africa, and the Middle East, from the 1940s to 1991. It is also a story of illegal immigration into Palestine and later into Israel, largely funded by American Jewish organizations who also provided personnel to assist with the operations. In the first phase from the mid-1940s to 1948 the support was for Palestinian Jewish clandestine operations, while during the second phase support was for the government of Israel and the Mossad. The key organizations involved in these operations were the American Jewish Joint Distribution Committee and the Hebrew Immigrant Aid Society. The work is based on personal insight into the American operations – interviews with Shaul Avigur's daughter clarify his role in Palestinian illegal immigration and the founding of Mossad Aliyeh Beth, the forerunner of the Mossad. The organization primarily stood for the illegal immigration operatives organization and Aliyeh Beth and Mossad were used interchangeably. The Aliyeh Beth was dissolved in 1951, being no longer required in independent Israel, though the new Mossad carried on its secret immigration functions, largely in North Africa and the Middle East. The private American Jewish organizations co-operated with the new Mossad and often provided a cover as well as finance for its immigration work. The study is divided into three parts: part one deals with the first rescues, which were largely concerned with illegal emigration from occupied Europe and the Eastern European states; part two deals with European operations between 1945 and 1950, being largely an operation based on rescuing displaced persons from German-occupied Europe and then the Russian-dominated Eastern states; part three deals with operations in the Middle East and North Africa. The work has numerous references to the Mossad throughout the text and shows its development over the years though the study is restricted to its operations in the rescue of Jewish communities in danger. In addition to the European operations the role of the Mossad is also considered in relation to emigration from Morocco, Egypt, Iraq, Syria and Ethiopia, and delicate negotiations in Romania to secure the release of some 300,000 Jews in return for compensation, most of which was retained by Ceausescu in Swiss bank accounts probably totalling $200 million. The writer has produced an authoritative account of the illegal migration of the threatened Jewish communities to Palestine and Israel, based on personal knowledge, interviews with significant personages, and access to archival material. At the same time the work is extremely readable and provides a useful study of one phase of the operations of the Mossad, significant because it was the reason for its founding and its success in these operations were partly responsible for the reputation that it gained for daring exploits. However, the work is also important for the study of the contribution of private Jewish organizations in these operations.

Anti-Nazi Operations

106 The last Nazi: the life and times of Joseph Mengele.
Gerald Astor.   New York: Donald I. Fine, 1985. 385p. bibliog.

An account, by an investigative journalist, of the life of Mengele, including his success in evading the clutches of Nazi-hunters and the discovery of his grave in Brazil in 1985. Astor includes references to the Mossad in the post-war quest to bring Mengele to justice.

107 Israel: a personal history.
David Ben-Gurion.   London: New English Library, 1971. 862p. maps.

An illustrated account by David Ben-Gurion of the creation of the modern State of Israel. He begins with a brief historical introduction, pioneering Jewish settlement at the beginning of the twentieth century, the period of the Mandate, and the story of the new state up to the time of writing. There are scattered brief references of relevance throughout the text but the main section of interest is Chapter Seven, 'The Trial of Adolf Eichmann' (p. 573-608), which deals in detail with the trial, presenting both defence and prosecution arguments, and examines relations with Argentina following the kidnap of Eichmann by a team from the Mossad.

108 The house on Garibaldi Street.
Isser Harel.   New York: Viking Press, 1975. 296p.

Harel gives an account of the complete operation mounted to trace, kidnap, and bring to trial Adolf Eichmann. He covers the detailed planning of the operation, the training of the Mossad team and the operation itself, including the painstaking work involved in tracing the whereabouts of Eichmann, the kidnap, and the justice process. The author was the former head of the Mossad and Israel's secret services. He also makes references to near misses in the hunt for Josef Mengele.

Anti-Nazi Operations

109 **The Mengele mystery; as new revelations multiply, the question remains: is this the Nazi doctor?**
Pico Iyer. *Time*, vol. 125 (24 June 1985), p. 38-44.
Iyer's article covers the discovery of the remains of Josef Mengele in a graveyard in Embu, Brazil, in June 1985, and discusses Mengele's life in Brazil, the forensic evidence from the remains, and evidence from associates of Mengele in his new life. It also includes a consideration of the Mossad operation to locate Mengele with three near misses in Ascunción, Paraguay, São Paulo, and on the Paraguayan–Brazilian border.

110 **Eichmann in my hands.**
Peter Z. Malkin, with Harry Stein.   New York: Warner Books, 1990. 272p.
An extremely detailed account of the clandestine Mossad operation to seize Adolf Eichmann in Argentina in 1960, the 1961 trial in Israel, and his execution in 1962. The account is in the form of a memoir from Malkin who was a member of the Mossad team that carried out the abduction. He joined the Haganah in 1939 and served with the Mossad from 1950 to 1976. He includes material on Mossad tradecraft, and a large amount of biographical data on Adolf Eichmann and on Malkin himself.

111 **Martin Bormann: Nazi in exile.**
Paul Manning.   Syracuse, New Jersey: Lyle Stuart, 1981. 302p.
Manning's controversial account of Bormann's supposed escape to South America following the Second World War contains numerous references to the Argentinian secret police, the CIA, and the Mossad. The work suffers from a lack of references and annotations but it is indexed.

112 **The capture of Adolf Eichmann.**
Moshe Pearlman.   London: Weidenfeld & Nicolson, 1961. 179p.
Pearlman relates the story of the Mossad operation to track down and capture Adolf Eichmann. The team had tracked Eichmann for a number of months before locating him in Argentina and engineering a kidnapping in order to bring him to trial in Israel for his part in the Holocaust.

113 **Mengele: the complete story.**
Gerald Posner, John Ware.   London: Queen Anne Press; New York: McGraw Hill, 1986. 364p. bibliog.
This biography of Mengele was based on unrestricted access to Mengele's family papers and diaries. The role of the Mossad in the hunt for Mengele and other Nazis is considered and there are numerous references to the Mossad. However, Chapter 7 'Operation Mengele' (p. 133-47) is the main section of relevance.

Arab–Israeli Wars

114 **The Ramadan war, 1973.**
   Hassan El Badri, Taha El-Magdoub, Mohammed El din Zohdy.
   Dun Loring, Virginia: T. N. Dupuy Associates, 1979. 239p. maps.
   bibliog. (First published in Arabic. Cairo: United Company for
   Publishing & Distribution, 1974).

The authors were three Arab generals involved in the October 1973 war against Israel. The book provides a detailed description and analysis of preparations for, and conduct of, the Ramadan – or Yom Kippur – war. The relevant section of the coverage is that related to the strategy of strategic and political misinformation waged by the Arabs and fed to Israeli intelligence. The problem for the Israeli strategists and politicians was the differing interpretations placed on the data by Israeli Military Intelligence and the Mossad; the latter perceived the real threat posed by Egyptian and Syrian troop movements and propaganda.

115 **Story of my life.**
   Moshe Dayan. London: Weidenfeld & Nicolson, 1976. 534p.

This is the illustrated autobiography of one of the most charismatic figures in the history of the modern State of Israel. Since 1948 he has served as soldier, politician, and Prime Minister. The bulk of the work is concerned with the Arab–Israeli wars and the military campaigns, with some reference to the role of intelligence in this area, though the Mossad is not dealt with as a separate entity.

116 **Elusive victory: the Arab–Israeli wars 1947-1974.**
   T. N. Dupuy. London: Macdonald & Janes, 1978. 669p. maps.
   bibliog.

Dupuy's study of the Arab–Israeli wars from 1947 to 1974 covers the causes of the various wars, the military strength of the protagonists, strategy and tactics, and the broader international political background and consequences. The work is included here because of the intelligence problems associated with the Yom Kippur war and the differing interpretations of data by the Mossad and Israeli Military Intelligence. The situation was further complicated by the inability of the government to act on the intelligence gathered; this resulted in initial setbacks for the Israeli forces.

117   **War, strategy and intelligence.**
Michael I. Handel.   London: Cass & Co., 1989. 500p. bibliog.
An excellent collection of material on different aspects of warfare, ranging from strategic surprise at the outset of hostilities to the complexities of the termination of the conflicts. The work includes coverage of the various Arab–Israeli wars and the role of the various intelligence services, including the Mossad, in these conflicts.

118   **Israel's fateful decisions.**
Yehashofat Harkabi.   London: I. B. Tauris, 1988. 246p.
A scholarly examination of Palestinian–Israeli relations and Israeli policies towards the Palestinians. A highly critical examination of the Likud party organization and the Premiership of Menachen Begin which concludes that their policies have, as their likely outcome, Israeli national suicide. Harkabi argues that some form of moderation of each side's basic goals must be found if a mutual disaster is to be avoided. The work has frequent references to past activities of the Jewish and Arab underground movements, intelligence gathering, the Lebanese civil war, the Israeli invasion of Lebanon in 1982, the Palestine Liberation Organization, Israeli military intelligence and deception strategy. The Mossad figures extensively in respect of the situation in the Lebanon.

119   **The road to Ramadan.**
Mohamed Heikal.   London: Collins, 1975. 285p.
The author was a journalist, editor of *Al Akram*, and one-time Egyptian Minister of Information. This illustrated work presents an Egyptian Arab viewpoint of the preparations for the Ramadan or Yom Kippur war of 1973 and of the political aftermath. It is included here because of the intelligence aspects and the surprise expressed by the Arabs at the lack of Israeli preparedness for the attack. Although there is no explanation of the associated events in Israel resulting in action the work is useful for an account of pertinent events through Arab eyes.

120   **Surprise attack: the victim's perspective.**
Ephraim Kam.   Cambridge, Massachusetts: Harvard University Press, 1988. 266p.
This is a detailed, authoritative review and analysis of the subject of surprise attack at the strategic level from the standpoint of the victim. It is a fundamental examination of the theory and practice of strategic intelligence and its role in the national decision-making process. It has been included because of the assessment of the Yom Kippur war and the differing interpretation of intelligence data by Israeli Military Intelligence and the Mossad.

121   **The road to war 1967: the origins of the Arab–Israeli conflict.**
Walter Laqueur.   London: Weidenfeld & Nicolson, 1968. 358p. bibliog.
A study of the Arab–Israeli conflict and the events leading up to the June 1967 war which Israel won largely as a result of superior intelligence provided by the Mossad

Arab–Israeli Wars

and Israeli military intelligence. In respect of Syria, much of the military intelligence had been supplied by the Mossad agent Eli Cohen who had penetrated Syrian society and the military high command before his capture and execution in 1965.

122 The six days of Yad-Mordechai.
Margaret Larkin.   Tel Aviv: Ministry of Reference Publishing House, 1965. 343p. bibliog. (Published in 1963 in Hebrew).

A detailed account of the six days of resistance by Kibbutz Yad-Mordechai to Egyptian attack at the outset of the 1948 war. The work has numerous references to the Mossad but is not indexed.

123 Arab reach: the secret war against Israel.
Hoag Levins.   London: Sidgwick & Jackson; New York: Doubleday & Co., 1983. 324p. bibliog.

An account of Arab political and economic war against Israel using the vast income available from oil revenues. It includes Arab support for guerrilla forces, secret weapons programmes, and economic boycotts. There are numerous references to intelligence operations, including Israeli military intelligence and the Mossad. In terms of the Mossad, reference is made to the involvement of the agency in the setting up of bogus companies in Cyprus to handle commercial trade to and from Israel to circumvent the Arab boycott. The author also considers Israel's attempt to obtain nuclear weapons, in which the Mossad had a major role, and the dangers of nuclear proliferation in the Middle East.

124 The Arab–Israeli war, October 1973: background and events.
Elizabeth Monroe.   London: Institute of Strategic Studies, 1975. 35p. (Adelphi Papers, no. 111).

Amongst the topics covered are the Arab misinformation campaign and the failure of the Israeli military and the politicians to correctly interpret the intelligence information provided by Mossad agents from Egypt.

125 Warriors for Jerusalem: the six days that changed the Middle East.
Donald Neff.   New York: Linden Press, 1984. 430p. bibliog.

A detailed review of events preceding, during, and following the Six Day war of 1967. The author considers the role of propaganda in this period and gives details of the output of Cairo Radio, misinformation tactics, Syrian guerrilla policy, and the role of the CIA and the Mossad.

126 Arab-guerrilla power 1967-1972.
Edgar O'Ballance.   London: Faber & Faber, 1974. 246p. maps.

The 1967 Arab–Israeli war left the Arab world humiliated and saw the development of Arab guerrilla power as a means of waging war against Israel. This work examines the growth of these movements, the politics of hijacking and assassination, and the response of the Israeli Defence Forces, Shin Bet and the Mossad to these campaigns. The misjudgements of the Fedayeen in Jordan are examined as these eventually led to a disastrous clash with the Jordanian army, their expulsion to the Lebanon, and the failure of the various movements to achieve an effective united front. O'Ballance points out that Israeli counter-intelligence measures had been effective and that the Israelis may be involved in counter-terrorism against the Palestinians, through the Mossad, pursuing a campaign of bombings and assassinations against guerrilla leaders.

127   **No victors, no vanquished: the Yom Kippur war.**
Edgar O'Ballance.   London: Barrie & Jenkins, 1979. 370p. maps.

This illustrated work is largely an account of the military aspects of the Yom Kippur war of 1973 which was a war of electronics, of immense material destruction, and saw the largest armoured battle since the Second World War, involving over two thousand tanks. The final section, entitled 'In retrospect' (p. 329-52), is a reassessment of the war and its aftermath. O'Ballance examines the intelligence issue, which many Israelis had blamed for their near defeat by Egypt and Syria, and concludes that the Mossad was efficient and had noted and reported Arab military activity and that the fault lay in the interpretation of the material by the strategists and politicians.

128   **From time immemorial: the origins of the Arab–Jewish conflict over Palestine.**
Joan Peters.   London; New York: Harper & Row, 1984. 601p. bibliog.

This detailed study deals with the origins of the Arab–Israeli conflict but concludes at the outbreak of the Second World War, thus predating the Mossad. However, there are references to NILI which is regarded by some writers as the precursor to the Mossad.

129   **Failures in National Intelligence estimates: the case of the Yom Kippur war.**
Avraham Shlaim.   *World Politics*, vol. 28, no. 3 (1976), p. 348-80.

The Yom Kippur war and the early successes of the Arabs were a major blow to Israeli national pride in addition to the cost paid in terms of lives and equipment. The surprise attack by Egypt and Israel was blamed on the failure of the intelligence services and this study discusses these factors. However, it is clear that Mossad field agents did provide intelligence on the Arab build-up as did Military Intelligence. The main problem was the faulty interpretation of the data by the strategists and politicians in Israel. These failures nearly led to Israel losing the war and caused a bitter post-mortem within Israeli intelligence circles once the war was over.

130   **The 1973 intelligence failure: a reconsideration.**
Janice Gross Stein.   *Jerusalem Quarterly*, no. 24 (Summer 1982), p. 41-54.

A detailed examination of the intelligence failure in respect of the Yom Kippur war and the consequences for the reputation of the intelligence community in Israel. The focus is primarily on Military Intelligence though the Mossad had been instrumental in providing data on the Egyptian build-up, data which was passed on to and confirmed by Military Intelligence. The object of this study is the analysis of the process of evaluation of intelligence, the interpretation of the data, and the use of the data in the political decision-making process. The study concludes that the question of attribution of blame to Military Intelligence or the Mossad is irrelevant as the real question is the value of such intelligence and the fact that it cannot protect against

Arab–Israeli Wars

surprise attack. However, the official report of the Agronat Commission set up to investigate the failure laid the blame on the domination of Military Intelligence and recommended that greater power should be given to the Mossad and to the Centre for Research and Strategic Planning (see item no. 30).

131 The Yom Kippur war.
Sunday Times Insight Team.   London: André Deutsch, 1975. 514p. maps.

This detailed and illustrated study of the Yom Kippur war of October 1973 by a team of *Sunday Times* journalists is based on interviews with Presidents Sadat and Asad, the chiefs of staff of the Arab armies, and the findings of the commission of inquiry into the reasons for Israel being unprepared for the war. The main section of interest is Chapter 6, 'Failures of intelligence' (p. 91-113), which deals with the gathering of intelligence data by the Mossad and army intelligence, and the failure by Israel to analyse the data correctly and foresee the attack. This was not a case of the intelligence agents failing to collect the data but of the infrastructure and the government failing to interpret it correctly, though Mossad had warned of the dangers and eventually obtained details of the Arab plans.

132 U.S. Intelligence Agencies and activities: the performance of the intelligence community, Part 2.
Washington, DC: Congressional Session 94-1, Sept. 11-12, 18, 25, 30; Oct. 7, 30-1, 1994. iv, 306p.

Part of a series of hearings by the Select Committee on Intelligence to oversee the activities of the United States Intelligence Services. This volume covers the agencies performance in monitoring foreign situations which may affect US foreign policy interests or national security. Of relevance here are the examination of aspects of the Yom Kippur war of 1973 and the failure of interpretation by Israeli Military Intelligence, the Mossad, and the Israeli politicians.

Palestine Liberation Organization

133 **Assignment murder: how Israel planned the killing of Arafat's right-hand man.**
Time, vol. 131 (2 May 1988), p. 36-8.
Khalil al-Wazir, better known as Abu Jihad, was assassinated by the Mossad on 16 April 1988 in Tunisia. This was a joint operation between the Mossad and the Israeli Defence Forces which included jamming of communications in the area by the Israeli Air Force.

134 **The quest for the Red Prince.**
Michel Bar-Zohar, Eitan Haber. London: Weidenfeld & Nicolson, 1983. 232p. bibliog.
This is an account of the Israeli hunt for Ali Hassan Salameh of the Palestine Liberation Organization who masterminded the Munich Olympic Games massacre. The Mossad led the operation and there are numerous references to the Palestine Liberation Organization, Arab terrorism, special covert operations, counter-intelligence activities, and the Israeli secret services in general.

135 **The PLO: the rise and fall of the Palestine Liberation Organization.**
Jillian Becker. London: Weidenfeld & Nicolson, 1984. 303p. map. bibliog.
This illustrated book is a study of the Palestine Liberation Organization, created as a weapon against Israel, which examines the structure, aims, and tactics of the PLO and its involvement in the conflict against Israel. There is no detailed study of the Mossad except for its activities following the massacre at the Munich Olympic Games and the account of the Israeli invasion of Lebanon in 1982. However, the work does deal with Israeli actions against the Palestinians in general and the Mossad were an integral part of these operations. It is also of value for providing a detailed study of the organization which has occupied most of the Mossad's attentions since 1964, and the splinter groups formed in later years.

Palestine Liberation Organization

136 **I can kill him now: inside Israel's decisions to hit – and not to hit Arafat.**
Lisa Beyer.   *Time International* (4 Oct. 1993), p. 64.

Beyer examines Israeli operations designed to either capture or kill Yasser Arafat, including an account of his evasion of capture by Shin Bet in December 1967. However, by 1972 Arafat was seen as a dangerous opponent especially as a result of the Munich Olympic Games massacre which resulted in a revenge operation being mounted by the Mossad. Arafat was excluded from the list of targets and the situation was not changed by the murder of a Mossad agent in Madrid in January 1973. Arafat also escaped being killed in the Lebanon during the 1982 invasion, largely because Israeli politicians had not reached a decision as to his execution.

137 **Deadly cycle of revenge.**
Derek Brown.   *Guardian* (London), (30 Oct. 1995), p. 8.

A report on the assassination of Fathi Shqaqi, founder of Islamic Jihad, in Malta in October 1995. Although Israel had not admitted responsibility it is considered to have been the work of the Mossad due to their reputation for ruthlessly using kidnap and murder to deal with enemies of the state.

138 **The Palestine Liberation Organization: people, power and politics.**
Helena Cobban.   Cambridge, England: Cambridge University Press, 1984. 305p. bibliog.

The author was a correspondent in Beirut from 1976 to 1981 and this work is a comprehensive political analysis of the Palestine Liberation Organization based on first-hand observations and documentary sources not used before in Western accounts of the PLO. The work also deals in depth with Al Fatah and its relationship with the PLO and the resistance movement within the occupied territories. The work is not indexed and the reader has to use the detailed contents list to identify incidents in which the Mossad were involved, an exercise which does require some knowledge of events. It is, however, an authoritative study of the PLO, its mainstream operations, and its terrorist activities, together with the Israeli response.

139 **Green March, Black September.**
John K. Cooley.   London: Cass, 1973. 263p. bibliog.

Cooley begins by tracing the early history of the Palestinians, illegal Jewish immigration, the creation of an Arab diaspora, the politics and culture of despair, and the rise of Palestinian guerrilla movements. This forms the core of the book and the author begins by considering their ideologies, the differences between the groups, and the development of relationships with other international terrorist organizations. Chapters 6 and 7 (p. 87-156) deal with the Palestinian guerrilla movements and their activities, particularly Black September, and the response of the Israeli intelligence services and secret services with a campaign of counter-violence. The massacre at the Munich Olympic Games and the Palestinian letter bomb campaign are dealt with at some length, and there is a brief consideration of the Israeli response.

Palestine Liberation Organization

140 Black September: its short, violent history.
Christopher Dobson. London: Hale, 1975. 192p.

This illustrated work deals with the structure, background and activities of Black September, and the threat posed to Israel and the Western world. Dobson examines the pattern of Black September activity, the massacre at the Munich Olympic Games, the campaign of hijacking and letter bombs, and links with other terrorist groups such as the Japanese Red Army and Baader-Meinhof. He also recounts the various responses of Israel to this terror campaign, most of which involved the Mossad and Shin Bet. The writer was a specialist in Middle East affairs for the London *Sunday Telegraph* and some of the material appeared first as newspaper articles in 1973.

141 Operation Peace for Galilee: the Israeli–PLO war in Lebanon.
Richard A. Gabriel. New York: Will & Wang, 1984. 242p.

Gabriel's scholarly review of the 1982 war in Lebanon is based on thousands of interviews with soldiers, guerrillas, and civilians on both sides. This work focuses largely on military events which are presented in an authoritative manner. However, there are numerous references to personalities and organizations such as Al Fatah, George Habash, the Palestine Liberation Organization, the Phalange, Stern Gang, the Mossad, counter-terrorism units, and guerrilla warfare.

142 The blood of Israel: the massacre of Israeli athletes in the 1972 Olympics.
Serge Groussard. New York: Morrow & Co., 1975. 464p.

A comprehensive account of the massacre of eleven Israeli athletes at the Munich Olympic Games by members of Black September. Groussard covers the operation itself, negotiations held with the terrorists, and the actions of the German authorities which resulted in shooting at the airport and deaths on both sides. He also deals with the Israeli reactions to the incident and the decision by the politicians to set up a team to track down the members of Black September and to exact revenge for the massacre. The eventual outcome was the killing of ten of the Black September members involved in the operation.

143 Arafat: terrorist or peacemaker?
Alan Hart. London: Sidgwick & Jackson, 1984. 480p. bibliog.

An authoritative, sympathetic account of the development of Yasser Arafat, leader of the Palestinian Liberation Organization, as a seeker of a peaceful solution to the Palestinian conflict. The work has numerous references to Algeria, Black September, Al Fatah, guerrilla warfare, the Stern Gang, and the Mossad.

144 The gun and the olive branch: the roots of violence in the Middle East.
David Hirst. London: Faber, 1977. 367p.

This excellent work deals with violence in the Middle East which had its roots in the 1880s when the Arabs were first driven off their lands by the first Jewish immigrant settlers in Palestine. The first part of the book is outside the present study except for setting the context of what was to follow. The work seeks to demonstrate that Arab violence, despite its fanaticism, can be viewed as a response to repeated aggression over a number of years, with the Israeli response seen as inevitable counter-violence.

Palestine Liberation Organization

Hirst also deals with the Munich Olympic Games massacre, Israeli actions against Black September, and with illegal immigration into Palestine from Europe during and after the Second World War – immigration which was organized by the forerunner of the Mossad. This work by the Middle East correspondent of the *Guardian* presents an extremely pessimistic assessment of the future.

145 Hunting Black September: now it can be told.
Newsweek, vol. 122 (6 Dec. 1993), p. 35.

The results of an interview, conducted in 1992, with Aharon Yariv, former adviser on terrorism to Golda Meir. The interview covers the Mossad operations to track down the members of Black September involved in the murder of eleven Israeli athletes at the Munich Olympic Games.

146 My home, my land: a narrative of the Palestinian struggle.
Abu Iyad, Eric Rouleau. New York: Times Books, 1981. 235p.

This autobiography of Abu Iyad, former deputy leader of Al Fatah, traces his story from exile after the 1948 creation of the State of Israel. Iyad had come full circle, however, for he became an advocate of a democratic multi-national Palestine rather than an advocate of terrorism. The authors deal with the Munich Olympic Games massacre and the Israeli response, with the bombing of refugee camps in Syria and Lebanon, and an intensification of the counter-terrorist war with a campaign of letter bombs and assassinations mounted by Mossad. Success was not always with the Mossad as Black September assassinated one of their leading agents, Baruch Cohen, in Madrid on 28 January 1973, thus causing the dismantling of the complete Israeli network in Spain. This aspect of the terrorist and counter-terrorist campaigns is largely dealt with in the chapter entitled 'The shadow war' (p. 97-120).

147 My people shall live: an autobiography of a revolutionary.
Leila Khaled. London: Hodder & Stoughton, 1973. 223p.

This illustrated autobiography was written as a result of interviews with Leila Khaled and notes provided by her, as well as published and unpublished material. The account was given to George Hajjar in July 1971 and it is from this basis that the book has been written. Leila Khaled was a member of the Popular Front for the Liberation of Palestine (PFLP), involved in the successful hijack of a TWA aircraft in 1969, and an unsuccessful hijack of an El Al aircraft in 1970 which resulted in her being arrested, tried, and imprisoned in Great Britain. She was released as part of an exchange deal in 1971. The book traces Leila's life from the 1948 Arab–Israeli war and concludes with the expulsion of the Palestinians from Jordan in 1973. There are no direct references to the Mossad but many to Israel's actions against the PFLP, and also to the perceived treachery of other Arab states such as Egypt and Jordan.

148 Inside the PLO: covert units, secret funds and the war against Israel and the United States.
Neil C. Livingstone, D. Halevy. New York: Morrow & Co., 1990. 336p. bibliog.

After expulsion from the Lebanon in 1982 the Palestine Liberation Organization seemed to be in eclipse but it rose from the ashes and became stronger than before. At the time that the book was written the PLO was in direct dialogue with the United

States and Yasser Arafat was accorded the treatment normally reserved for a head of state. This work probes behind the diplomatic breakthrough to record details of the rise of the PLO, its infrastructure, and its activities, both as an instrument of terror and a multinational corporation. The authors also provide details as to the PLO's finances, the existence of Yassar Arafat's secret funds, an inventory of covert units and terrorist cells, and an update on the organization's role in the Intifada. There are references to the Mossad throughout the text, but particularly in relation to Abu Nidal and the 'hit list' of terrorists wanted by Mossad for activities against the Jewish state.

149   **A message from Mossad.**
Economist, vol. 307, no. 7547 (23 April 1988), p. 42-3.

An explanation of the extremely sophisticated operation mounted by the Mossad to assassinate Abu Jihad or Khalil Wazir of the Palestine Liberation Organization. The resources behind the Mossad operation are also discussed.

150   **Revolutionary warfare in the Middle East: the Israelis vs the Fedayeen.**
Bard E. O'Neill.   Boulder, Colorado: Paladin Press, 1974. 140p.

O'Neill's account of the struggle between Israel and the Palestinian guerrillas over a period of years concentrates mainly on Israeli responses to terrorist attacks on Israeli interests and Israeli citizens. The full range of responses are covered from those of the Israeli Defence Forces, military intelligence, Shin Bet and the Mossad.

151   **Assassination of PLO man leaves trail of shadows.**
Jonathan Randal.   *Guardian* (London), (13 July 1992), p. 9.

An account of the assassination of Atef Bseiso, head of intelligence operations for the PLO, in June 1992 by Mossad agents. It is also possible, however, that the killing was carried out by the Palestinian, Sabri Nanna, regarded by the United States as the most dangerous terrorist in the world.

152   **Guerrillas for Palestine.**
Riad El-Rayyes, Dunia Nahas.   London: Croom Helm, 1976. 155p.

This is largely an account of the commando operations of the Palestinian movements and the structure of the various groups that have emerged, such as the Popular Front for the Liberation of Palestine, Al Fatah, and Black September. The authors also consider the political aspects of each of the organizations, and profiles are provided of the major personalities in the movements. In considering Israel's response to the activities of groups such as Black September, the authors conclude that the actions served to expose the counter-violence of the Mossad and Shin Bet, and the fact that Israel was responsible for state terrorism. Some of the Israeli actions against Black September are briefly considered. The book is based on contacts, and interviews with leaders and planners of the various commando movements within the Palestinian resistance. There is a useful glossary.

153   **Freedom will be the death of him.**
David Rose.   *Observer* (London), no. 10592 (16 Oct. 1994), p. 6.

This article speculates on the future of Ismael Sowan who was due to be released from a British jail in December 1994 and repatriated to Israel. Sowan was a former Mossad

Palestine Liberation Organization

agent and PLO activist, jailed after showing authorities a Palestinian arms cache, and believed to be part of secret Mossad operations in Britain. The writer felt that Sowan's fate was to be execution at the hands of fellow Arabs on his release. Sowan himself maintained that Israel had always promised to obtain his release and had failed to keep its promise.

154 Master of mystery and murder; for the shadowy Abu Nidal, terror is a way of life.
George Russell. *Time*, vol. 127 (13 Jan. 1986), p. 31-2.

An assessment of the case of Abu Nidal, leader of Al Fatah, and his terrorist attacks against Israeli targets and fellow Arabs who favoured compromise with Israel. However, there was speculation that Abu Nidal was in reality a Mossad agent, a charge levied by Yasser Arafat in 1982.

155 Fedayeen: the story of the Palestinian guerrillas.
Zeev Schiff, Raphael Rothstein.   London: Vallentine Mitchell, 1972. 252p.

This is primarily a study of the Fedayeen, the organization of Palestinian guerrillas responsible for a range of terrorist activities and assassinations throughout the Middle East and Europe. The work covers all aspects of the movement: origins, politics, military activities, ideology, the campaign against Israel, and Russian support for its activities. The work has no direct references to the Mossad but it deals with the killings at Lod airport and the Munich Olympic Games both of which were to result in direct action by the Mossad.

156 Abu Nidal: a gun for hire.
Patrick Seale.   London: Hutchinson; New York: Random House, 1992. 339p.

Seale's authoritative account of the career of Abu Nidal, the most notorious of the Arab terrorists, is also a guide to the intricacies of Middle East politics over a quarter of a century. The work is based partly on exclusive and extensive access to defectors from Abu Nidal's organization and examines the structure of the organization and the sources of finance, including Abu Nidal's own personal fortune. Although Abu Nidal is ostensibly a die-hard Palestinian nationalist avowed to destroy the State of Israel, many of his activities have been directed against fellow nationalists bent on pursuing a more moderate line over Israel. The success of the operations directed against fellow Arabs has also led to the proposition that Nidal was really a tool of Israeli intelligence, an idea reinforced by Israel's apparent reluctance to retaliate against Abu Nidal, in spite of his attacks on Jewish targets. There are numerous references to the Mossad throughout the text, particularly with regard to the infiltration of the Palestinian organization and possible links between the two organizations, supported by hearsay evidence from Jordanian, German and French sources. An unattributed French government expert on terrorism is quoted as telling the author in an interview that 'If Abu Nidal himself is not an Israeli agent then two or three of his senior people most certainly are. Nothing else can explain some of his operations. But the tracks are well covered and proof will be hard to find'. In addition to this evidence the work also examines the lack of Israeli action against Abu Nidal. It is pointed out that since the late 1960s, and the Israeli's free hand in the Lebanon, retribution has always followed any Palestinian guerrilla activity, or pre-emptive attacks have been launched.

Palestine Liberation Organization

However, despite knowing the exact location of Abu Nidal's camp east of Sidon no major attack had been launched by the Israeli Air Force, nor had the organization been seriously hit by Mossad assassination squads, despite their successful operations elsewhere. Further suspicions are voiced by Seale in relation to Nidal's lack of activity in the occupied territories and his attempts to sabotage the effectiveness of Palestinian activities, and in the Lebanon where Nidal deliberately fuelled dissent between Amal and Hizballah. He concludes that Nidal had always done deals with various states for protection as he could not have survived without state cover. 'Israel could easily end Abu Nidal's career if it chose to do so. But it had not done so. Why? Was he still useful? Abu Nidal needed immunity. Israel needed his services'.

157   I regret nothing but the time for killing is over.
Mike Theodoulou.   *Observer* (London), no. 10538 (3 Oct. 1993), p. 18.

An interview with Ian Davison, a Briton, who had been jailed in Cyprus for the murder of Mossad agents on behalf of the PLO. The interview reveals that Davison had no regrets about his terrorist activities but now supported the peace deal with Israel negotiated by Yasser Arafat.

158   Hit team: the exciting story of Israel's strike against Arab terrorists in Europe.
David C. Tinnin, Christopher Dag.   London: Weidenfeld & Nicolson, 1976. 196p.

An account of the actions taken by the Israeli government, largely through the Mossad, to retaliate against the serious terrorist attacks and letter bomb campaigns mounted by Palestinian guerrillas. The authors record the series of operations mounted to track down and execute Palestinian guerrillas and their sympathizers, including the use of letter bombs to exact revenge. The existence of such a hit team was denied by the Israeli government.

Foreign Incursions

General

159   **The unnatural alliance.**
James Adams.   London: Quartet, 1984. 218p. bibliog.

The story of the growing interdependence of South Africa and Israel as outcast nations in the international arena. Adams includes a study of the sharing of intelligence data between 1975 and 1989, arms production and technical data, counter-terrorism, and the role of the Mossad as a trainer of South African forces and supplier of intelligence data.

160   **Israel's military relationship with Ecuador and Argentina.**
Bishara Bahbah.   *Journal of Palestine Studies,* vol. 15, no. 2 (1986), p. 76-101.

A discussion of Israel's military connections with Ecuador and Argentina, including the scale of the operation and the motives for Israeli involvement. In the case of Ecuador the possible role of Haim Topel, a former Mossad agent, in securing military contacts is briefly considered.

161   **The Israeli connection: who Israel arms and why.**
Benjamin Beit-Hallahmi.   New York: Random House, 1987. 289p. bibliog.

A detailed review of Israel's role as an arms dealer and military and intelligence security trainer for nations of the developing world. The author discusses relations with ten Far Eastern, nineteen African, and nine Latin American countries, including intelligence exchanges and the training of internal security forces of client countries. The Mossad is an active participant in these areas. The story told is one of intrigue and covert action, showing that in Israel's struggle to survive it will align itself with some of the most reactionary regimes in the world, and much stress is laid on the secret alliance with South Africa.

Foreign Incursions. General

162   **Libyan sandstorm.**
      John K. Cooley.   New York: Holt, Rinehart & Winston, 1982. 320p.
Cooley's story of Libya since the 1969 revolution has numerous references to subversion and intelligence organizations, including the Mossad.

163   **Death in Paris; mystery surrounds the assassination of a PLO leader on a secret mission.**
      Time International (22 June 1992), p. 12.
A report on the assassination of Atef Bseiso, a senior intelligence officer for the PLO, in Paris. PLO officials blamed the Mossad but Abu Nidal was another candidate. The smoothness of the operation led to rumours that French intelligence, with whom he was due to meet, had tipped off the killers about his movements.

164   **Land for peace? Shultz wings in as a familiar debate rages.**
      William R. Doerner.   *Time* (29 Feb. 1988), p. 50.
An account of George Shultz's peace mission in the Middle East and the regional background to that mission. Doerner includes a consideration of the Mossad operation to assassinate three Al Fatah agents in Limassol, Cyprus, in February 1988, by means of a remote-control bomb. The Al Fatah mission was to buy a ferry to transport 130 Palestinian refugees expelled by Israel to Haifa, and this was damaged in a separate raid. Israel did not conceal its role in the bombing of the ferry but denied responsibility for the car bombing.

165   **Israel's diplomatic offensive in Africa: the case of Zaïre.**
      N. Dropkin.   *Transafrica Forum*, vol. 9, no. 1 (1992), p. 15-26.
An examination of the reasons behind Zaïre's restoration of diplomatic relations with Israel in 1982. Dropkin concludes that the motivation of President Mobutu was the preservation of his own position against the threat of armed challenge to his totalitarian rule. As Zaïre had been isolated by its traditional allies Mobutu was forced to turn to Israel for training of her military and security services; the latter involved the Mossad.

166   **Israelis to advise Chamorro's spies.**
      Bill Gertz.   *Insight*, vol. 6 (14 May 1990), p. 34.
Although this is a brief article, it is included because it details links between the Mossad and Nicaragua, and the part played by Israeli agents in the training of Nicaraguan internal security forces.

167   **Gadaffi courts Israel in $1 bn diplomacy drive.**
      Andrew Hogg.   *Sunday Times* (London), no. 8816 (8 Aug. 1993), p. 15.
Hogg discusses efforts by Colonel Gadaffi to enlist the support of Israel to improve Libya's image in the United States. The deal involved a former Mossad agent, Yaacov Nimrodi, and Adnan Khashoggi, a Saudi arms dealer, apparently backed by Shimon Peres.

Foreign Incursions. Operations against Iraq

168   **The Iranian triangle: the untold story of Israel's role in the Iran–Contra affair.**
Samuel Segev.   New York: The Free Press, 1988. 340p. bibliog.

This is a detailed, authoritative account of the role of Israel in the Iran–Contra affair. The work begins by exploring the history of the clandestine relationship between Israel and Iran which had begun in the 1950s and even continued on an informal basis during the period of the Khomeini revolution. There are numerous references to the Mossad, Arafat, Syria, Iraq, the Palestine Liberation Organization, the Pollard espionage affair, and religious extremism. The work is based on official records, transcripts of meetings, unpublished primary sources, and interviews with key officials.

169   **Pontiff: inside the Vatican – behind today's sensational headlines.**
Gordon Thomas, Max Morgan-Wilts.   New York: Doubleday & Co., 1983. 461p.

A narrative of Vatican events, starting from the time of Pope Paul VI and including the attempted assassination of Pope John Paul II. There are numerous references to conspiracies, assassinations, and secret communications with Libya and Syria, with references to the operations of the Mossad in those countries.

Operations against Iraq

170   **Bull's eye: the assassination and life of supergun inventor Gerald Bull.**
James Adams.   New York: Random House, 1992. 371p.

The activities of Bull range wider than his associations with Iraq and the supergun affair. However, it was this invention that caused his death on 22 March 1990, ostensibly at the hands of the Mossad.

171   **Operation Babylon: the story of the rescues of the Jews of Iraq.**
Shlomo Hillal.   New York: Doubleday, 1987. 301p. (Originally published in Israel, in Hebrew, by Edani Publishing, 1985).

This work is an excellent account of the history of the escape of some 120,000 Jews from Iraq between 1946 and 1950. The work is based on personal recollections of the author, declassified private records of the Haganah, and Israeli and British Foreign Ministry records. The work has numerous incidental references to the Mossad and its role in the operation during the latter stages, though much of the motivation and infrastructure came from within the Iraqi-Jewish community. The work also has an unannotated glossary of terms.

Foreign Incursions. Operations against Iraq

172 **The man with the golden gun.**
D'Arcy Jenish. *Maclean's*, vol. 104, no. 16 (27 April 1991), p. 44-5.

A study of the career of Gerald Bull, the Canadian weapons developer, who was involved in developing the Iraqi supergun and allegedly murdered by Mossad agents in March 1990. The gun was designed to hit targets at a range of 1,000 miles. The article also deals with the British companies manufacturing components for the gun and their seizure by customs officials. Bull had also been instrumental in supplying South Africa with howitzers and shells and some of these also found their way to Iraq.

173 **Arms and the man: Dr. Gerald Bull, Iraq and the supergun.**
William Lowther. Novato, California: Presido Press, 1991. 298p.

An illustrated account of Bull's associations with Iraq and his involvement in the design of a supergun prior to the outbreak of the Gulf War. Bull was murdered on 22 March 1990 and it is thought that the operation may have been mounted by the Mossad.

174 **Bullseye – one reactor.**
Don McKinnon. San Diego, California: House of Hits Publishing, 1987. 200p. bibliog.

This is an account of the Israeli raid on Iraq's nuclear reactor which took place on 7 June 1981. The Mossad had been charged with the task of determining the Arab capability to produce nuclear and chemical weapons and provided intelligence for the raid. This was provided largely from agents based within Iraq and their role is examined in relation to the success of the operation. The work is based on interviews and secondary sources.

175 **First strike: the exclusive story of how Israel foiled Iraq's attempts to get the bomb.**
Shlomo Nakdiman. New York: Simon & Schuster, 1987. 353p. bibliog.

A journalistic account of Israel's surprise attack on Iraq's nuclear reactor on 7 June 1981. There are numerous references to the intelligence operation of the Mossad in preparing the way for the operation. The work is based on classified intelligence documents, interviews, and a detailed review of world press reports.

176 **Two minutes over Baghdad.**
Amos Perlmutter, Michael I. Handel, Uri Bar-Joseph. London: Vallentine Mitchell, 1982. 191p.

An account of the raid by the Israeli Air Force on the Iraqi nuclear reactor at Ossirah. Intelligence for the raid had been provided by Mossad agents who had been engaged in an operation to assess the nuclear capabilities of all the Arab countries.

177 **Circle of fear.**
Hussein Sumaida. London: Hale, 1992. 304p.

The author was once a member of Iraq's secret service, a leading member of the Ba'ath party, and a member of Iraq's political élite. When he was in London in 1984, however, Sumaida volunteered his services to the Mossad as a means of working

Foreign Incursions. Lebanese incursions

against Saddam Hussein. He operated both in Britain and in Belgium where his father was ambassador. The intelligence provided by Sumaida included data on the terrorist activities of the Iraqi Mukhbarat agents against Kurds in Europe, the Bull supergun development, and other Arabs in the United Kingdom. Sumaida was suspected by his father and so he decided to volunteer information to a Mukhbarat agent in Brussels in the hope of covering the escapade as a terrible mistake rather than a deliberate act. Sumaida was not imprisoned by the Iraqis but pardoned by Saddam Hussein provided that he worked for Mukhbarat. A large section of the book covers Sumaida's training with Mukhbarat, his studies and spying activities at Baghdad University, the activities of the Iraqi secret service, and his determination to leave Iraq. This section also deals incidentally with activities of the Mossad where they were known through contact with senior officials in Iraq, and with Iraq's nuclear capability. In 1990 Sumaida escaped to the Yemen, where he went to the United States embassy to seek asylum, but with no result; he then made his way to Canada via Germany and thence to the United Kingdom, pursued by Iraqi agents. He was returned to Canada and, at the time of writing, his case for asylum was still being considered.

Lebanese incursions

178 Onward Christian diplomats.
Craig S. Karpel. *The New Republic*, vol. 191 (3 Sept. 1984), p. 21-8.

An assessment of relations between Israel and Lebanese Christians, including the establishment of the Lebanese Christian Agency office in Jerusalem under the protection of the Mossad. Karpel also deals with the Christian–Muslim–Syrian power struggle in Lebanon and the continued presence of Israel in South Lebanon.

179 A general loses his case.
James Kelly. *Time*, vol. 125 (4 Feb. 1985), p. 64-6.

An account of the libel case brought by Ariel Sharon against *Time* magazine regarding his involvement in the massacres at Sabra and Shatilla refugee camps. The case was lost by Sharon as the jury accepted that he had met secretly with Lebanese Phalangists prior to the massacre and was aware that a revenge attack was being planned to avenge the death of Bashir Gemayel. The account of one of these meetings was supplied to the *Time* reporter by an unidentified Israeli intelligence officer who had kept notes of the discussion. The magazine was, however, criticized for careless reporting and for inaccuracy with regard to some of the content of the story.

180 The covenant: love and death in Beirut.
Barbara Newman.   New York: Crown Publishers, 1989. 242p.

The story of Bashir Gemayel, assassinated President of Lebanon, by an American journalist who became his lover. There are references to the Mossad and its operations, particularly the assassination of Abu Jihad.

Foreign Incursions. Lebanese incursions

181 **The tragedy of Lebanon: Christian warlords, Israeli adventurers and American bunglers.**
Jonathan Randal. London: Hogarth Press, 1990. rev. ed. 381p. maps.

The author was a reporter for the *Washington Post* who had reported from the Lebanon since the civil war of 1975-76. This work analyses events in that country, ravaged by both internal strife and external pressures. It provides a study of Israeli policies towards the Lebanon, her liaison with the Christian warlords, the self-declared security zone following the invasion of 1982, and the political aftermath. There are references to the Mossad largely in relation to its involvement in providing intelligence prior to the invasion and its close connection with the Christian warlords and their forces.

182 **Israel's Lebanon war.**
Ze'ev Schiff, Ehud Ya'ari. London: Allen & Unwin, 1986. 330p. maps.

Two highly respected Israeli journalists examine the reasons why Israel invaded the Lebanon in 1982, the objectives of the Likud government, and the reasons why the invasion went wrong. The study is based on interviews with witnesses and high government officials in Jerusalem, Washington and Beirut; minutes of secret meetings; and classified letters and archives, including PLO files captured at Sidon and Beirut. The work is included here because of its coverage of clandestine operations in which the Mossad were involved, including negotiations with the Christian Phalange leader Bashir Gemayel, and subsequent support for the Phalangists which led to the massacres in Shatilla and Sabra refugee camps. The authors conclude that the invasion was a critical mistake by Israel as it has caused divisions within Israel, inflicted damage on Israel's world-wide image, failed to destroy the PLO, and left Lebanon in anarchy.

183 **Elusive security: the military and political geography of south Lebanon.**
C. H. Schofield. *GeoJournal*, vol. 31, no. 2 (1993), p. 149-61.

An examination of the historical background to Israel's security policies on her northern border which date back to the establishment of the Palestine Mandate. From the end of the First World War to the 1960s the policy was dominated by economic and environmental security but the following decades showed a growth in border security requirements in the face of military intervention from Lebanon. Following Israel's invasion of the Lebanon in 1982, intelligence for which was provided by the Mossad, an occupied security zone was established in south Lebanon and Schofield concludes that it was extremely unlikely that this territory would be relinquished, since that would undermine the possibility of permanent security in the area.

184 **Snowball: the story behind the Lebanon war.**
Simon Shiffer. Tel Aviv: Edonim Publishers, 1984.

185 **The verdict is guilty.**
William E. Smith. *Time*, vol. 121 (21 Feb. 1983), p. 26-33.

An examination of the massacres at Sabra and Shatilla refugee camps by Lebanese Phalangists and the subsequent report of the Israeli Commission of Inquiry. The report

Foreign Incursions. Relations with the United States and US Intelligence

made a distinction between direct and indirect involvement in the massacres, laying blame for direct involvement on the Phalangists, but attaching indirect blame to a number of Israeli Defence Force officers and Ministers, with the Defence Minister receiving the most damning criticism. It was determined that no action should be taken against the Director of the Mossad as he had only just taken up his post four days before the massacre.

186   **Dilemmas of security: politics, strategy and the Israeli experience in Lebanon.**
Avner Yaniv.   London; New York: Oxford University Press, 1987. 355p. bibliog.

A comprehensive account of the Israeli invasion of the Lebanon in 1982 and the repercussions. The work is based largely on interviews in Israel, Lebanon and the United States, and on published sources. The role of the Mossad in preparing the groundwork for the invasion is considered and its subsequent role following the invasion in dealings with the Christian warlords.

Relations with the United States and US Intelligence

187   **The eagle and the lion: tragedy of American–Iranian relations.**
Jonas A. Bill.   New Haven, Connecticut: Yale University Press, 1988. 520p. bibliog.

A scholarly review of United States–Iranian relations from the 1940s to the 1980s, with detailed coverage of the overthrow of Musaddiq in 1953, the overthrow of the Shah in 1979, the US hostage crisis and the ill-fated rescue attempt in 1980, together with the Iran–Contra affair of 1985 and 1986. There are numerous references to the intelligence-gathering activities of the Mossad and covert activities. The study is based on interviews in the United States and Iran, United States Embassy files in Teheran, Iranian sources, and archival material.

188   **Between Washington and Jerusalem.**
Wolf Blitzer.   London; New York: Oxford University Press, 1985. 259p.

This is a detailed study of United States and Israeli relationships based largely on interviews with policy-makers in both countries. Various major policy issues are examined to determine the nature of the relationship and there are references to co-operation between the CIA and the Mossad.

Foreign Incursions. Relations with the United States and US Intelligence

189   **Territory of lies: the exclusive story of Jonathan Jay Pollard: the American who spied on his country for Israel and how he was betrayed.**
Wolf Blitzer.   London; New York: Harper & Row, 1989. 336p. bibliog.

An excellent review and analysis of the case of Anne and Jonathan Pollard, the latter a US intelligence analyst imprisoned on charges of spying for Israel. It includes an account of the Israeli government's attempts to minimize the impact of this 'friendly espionage' case which had been engineered and controlled by the Mossad. The work is based on interviews with Pollard and his family, interviews with United States and Israeli officials, and transcripts of the trial.

190   **Ex-spy says U.S. indicted him for role in Pan-Am case; former Mossad agent claims mail-fraud case is a move to discredit him.**
Andrew Blum.   *National Law Journal*, vol. 18, no. 4 (25 Sept. 1995), p. A11.

An illustrated account of the prosecution of former Mossad agent and US government investigator Juval Aviv for mail fraud purely in order to discredit him. The claim is that Aviv used his Mossad experience as a defence expert for the airline with his report asserting that the terrorists used information about the CIA's protection of a Syrian heroin ring to evade airline security.

191   **The C. I. A.: a forgotten history.**
Walter Blum.   London; Atlantic Highlands, New Jersey: Zed Books, 1986. 428p.

Blum's extensive examination of CIA covert activities since the Second World War includes operations in the Middle East and co-operation between the CIA, the Mossad, and other Israeli intelligence services. The work is a hostile review and study of these operations.

192   **Dangerous liaison: the inside story of the US–Israeli covert relationship.**
Andrew Cockburn, Leslie Cockburn.   New York: Harper Collins, 1991. 416p.

This is an extremely detailed study and analysis of the co-operation between Israeli and American intelligence agencies and the influence that this relationship had on key developments in the Middle East. The work covers operations mounted by the Mossad on behalf of the United States where it could not be seen – or was not able – to have a direct presence; arms deals and anti-terrorist training of South American movements supported by the United States; and the US role in Israel's presumed acquisition of a nuclear capability.

Foreign Incursions. Relations with the United States and US Intelligence

193 Secret warriors: inside the covert military operations of the Reagan era.
Steve Emerson.   New York: G. P. Putnam's Sons, 1988. 256p.

An account by an investigative journalist of United States covert operations conducted during the Reagan administration. Emerson reveals details of clandestine operations carried out by a variety of deep-cover military elements. He includes coverage of various countries of the Middle East, including Israel and Iran, and the role of the Mossad as a partner in the region.

194 Deception: the invisible war between the KGB and the CIA.
Edward J. Epstein.   New York: Simon & Schuster, 1989. 335p. bibliog.

This work is an excellent historical investigation and analysis of deception from the First World War to 1988. It includes studies of CIA and KGB activity in the Middle East and the role of the Mossad as a close partner of the CIA in the region, often operating in areas which were difficult for the US agency.

195 They dare to speak out.
Paul Findley.   Westport, Connecticut: Lawrence Hill & Co., 1985. 362p. bibliog.

An examination of the Israeli lobby's all-pervasive influence on opinion leaders in the United States and the actions taken by the lobby against United States politicians who dared to criticize Israel. The Mossad is considered as a major player in actions against critics of Israel.

196 Mossad linked to WTC bomb suspect.
Robert I. Friedman.   *Village Voice*, vol. 38, no. 31 (3 Aug. 1993), p. 19.

Ahmad Ajaz had been arrested for conspiracy to bomb the World Trade Centre and there was some suspicion that he may have been a Mossad mole.

197 The unorthodox Rabbi.
Robert I. Friedman.   *Village Voice*, vol. 35, no. 34 (1990), p. 29-35.

Ronald Greenwald is both a Rabbi and the owner of an international commodities firm in New York. He campaigned on behalf of Anatoly Sharonsky and was being branded as a Mossad agent because of his activities.

198 Taking sides: America's secret relations with a militant Israel.
Stephen Green.   New York: Morrow & Co., 1984. 370p.

Green documents accounts of secret relations between the United States and Israel. He makes numerous references to intelligence and security matters, including relations with the Haganah, Israeli Military Intelligence, and the Mossad.

Foreign Incursions. Relations with the United States and US Intelligence

199 Pollard: the spy's legacy.
Bernard R. Henderson. New York: Alpha Books, 1988. 282p.

This is a plea for the reduction of sentences on Jonathan and Anne Pollard who were imprisoned for espionage on behalf of Israel. Henderson makes numerous references to the role of Israeli Military Intelligence and the Mossad who used the Pollards to obtain US defence technology secrets. The work is based upon biographical sketches of the personalities involved, and an extensive memoranda and letters by the Pollards and the author to the courts.

200 The price of power: Kissinger in the Nixon White House.
Seymour M. Hersh. New York: Simon & Schuster, 1983. 698p.

This is primarily an investigative journalist's account of Henry Kissinger's period in the White House, dealing with the Nixon Presidency and the background to Watergate. However, there is a broader coverage than US politics, and Hersh examines Kissinger's role in foreign affairs and his attempt to broker a peace settlement in the Middle East. There are numerous references to the Palestine Liberation Organization, Black September, the activities of the Mossad. The author also considers Israeli responses to Black September following a series of hijackings, the Munich Olympic Games massacre, and the letter bomb campaign.

201 Israel: foreign intelligence and security services.
Washington, DC: Central Intelligence Agency, 1976. [n.p.].

A secret, classified report on all branches of Israeli intelligence, including the Mossad. However, the material contained in the report was published in Iran in late 1979 following the seizure of the American Embassy in Teheran by Islamic militants in that same year. The report, and other material, was rescued from the embassy shredder and painstakingly pasted together by the militants. A copy exists in the Russell J. Bowen collection at Georgetown University, Washington, DC.

202 Israeli spies in the US.
Middle East Report, vol. 16 (Jan./Feb. 1986), p. 35-7. (Middle East Research and Information Project).

A brief overview of relations between Israeli and United States intelligence agencies, including the CIA and Mossad partnership since the 1950s.

203 Manhunt: the incredible pursuit of a CIA agent turned terrorist.
Peter Maas. New York: Random House, 1986. 301p. bibliog.

This work is an examination of the United States Justice Department's investigation and arrest of Edwin P. Wilson, a former CIA agent, who had been involved in illegal international trade and smuggling activities in support of Qadaffi and the Libyan regime. There are numerous references to the work of the Mossad in providing intelligence prior to the investigation. The work is based on official intelligence reports, court records, and interviews with involved personalities and officials.

Foreign Incursions. Relations with the United States and US Intelligence

204 **The Iran connection: secret teams and covert operations in the Reagan era.**
Jonathan Marshall, Peter Dale Scott, Jane Hunter.   Boston, Massachusetts: South End Press, 1987. 315p.

A detailed, critical account of the Iran–Contra affair as a logical progression of the long tradition of covert United States activities. The work has numerous incidental references to the Mossad.

205 **Casey: the lives and secrets of William J. Casey: from the OSS to the CIA.**
Joseph E. Persico.   London; New York: Penguin, 1990. 681p.

An authoritative biography of William J. Casey, with the emphasis on his intelligence service in the OSS in the Second World War, and as Director of the CIA under President Reagan from 1981 to 1987. It is interesting for its coverage of the Iran–Contra affair and the involvement of the Mossad in the operation.

206 **Triple trouble in Israel.**
Eliahu Salpeter.   *The New Leader*, vol. 70, no. 5 (March 1987), p. 5-7.

Salpeter examines three issues which were seriously affecting US–Israeli relations at the time of writing. The first was Israel's relations with South Africa in terms of arms supplies and the training of security forces. This was considered to be of least importance as Israel was well down the list of countries doing business with South Africa, including some of the Black African states. The second, far more serious, issue was Israel's role in the Iran arms sales affair, initially with David Kimche, a former high-ranking member of Mossad, as an intermediary, but a change of personnel led to Israel becoming more deeply involved in the Nicaragua–Contra side of the affair. The affair was regarded more seriously in the United States as the Israelis were more pragmatic regarding Khomeini as transient with, in the long run, Iran remaining a strategic ally against the Arabs. The third issue was the Jonathan Jay Pollard espionage affair; Israel tried to pass it off as a rogue operation but reactions in the United States caused Israel to set up a committee of inquiry into the affair.

207 **Jay Pollard's peculiar tale.**
Michael Satchell.   *U.S. News and World Report*, vol. 102 (1 June 1987), p. 23-5.

Satchell's account of the Pollard spying case in the United States describes his activities on behalf of Israel through the provision of defence technology secrets to the Mossad. The case strained relations between the two countries.

208 **Spying between friends: the Pollard verdict causes a wave of unease in Israel.**
William E. Smith.   *Time*, vol. 129 (16 March 1987), p. 44-5.

An examination of the Jonathan Jay Pollard affair and its effects on US–Israeli relations. The effects were serious: Israeli Defence Minister, Yitzhak Rabin, described it as a 'real disaster, a real wound in Israeli–US relations'. The case was regarded extremely seriously in the United States because of the volume and nature of the material stolen by Pollard which covered, amongst other topics, nuclear facilities in

Foreign Incursions. Relations with the United States and US Intelligence

Iraq and Pakistan, Soviet surface-to-air missile capabilities, and anti-aircraft facilities around the PLO headquarters in Tunisia. The article includes comments on the case from the Pollards.

209 Uproar over a spy: the Pollard case sparks new US–Israeli tensions.
William E. Smith.   *Time*, vol. 129 (23 March 1987), p. 30-3.

Primarily an examination of the Jonathan Jay Pollard espionage case in the United States, this article also includes a background survey of the Mossad as an organization. Initially Prime Minister Shamir refused to back an investigation into the scandal, maintaining that it was a rogue operation and that Israel had apologized sufficiently for the operation. The position taken by Shamir also angered American Jewish leaders who were disturbed by the refusal to take responsibility for the Mossad and Pollard's actions. Smith concludes that Israel's vaunted security apparatus seemed to be out of control with Shin Bet being under a cloud, the Mossad kidnapping of Mordechai Vananu, and the Iranian arms affair, with intelligence operations being run outside of established channels, and the extent of civilian political scrutiny.

210 Veil: the secret wars of the CIA 1981-1987.
Bob Woodward.   New York: Simon & Schuster, 1987. 543p. bibliog.

This is a highly controversial, detailed, and often indiscreet account of William Casey's period as director of the Central Intelligence Agency from 1981 to 1987. The work concentrates on covert operations and the deliberate by-passing of Congress and CIA policy guidelines in pursuit of his own objectives. Casey was an admirer of Israel and of the Mossad, being particularly impressed by the raid on Iraq's nuclear reactor on 7 June 1981, using plans supplied by the United States. However, within the CIA Israeli intelligence was regarded of being of little substance except for the satisfaction of Israeli political objectives, and with a reputation largely created by the media. Casey had to persuade operatives within the CIA that Mossad was credible as they had agents in three areas vital to United States interests: Lebanon, Syria and the Soviet Union. The Israeli invasion of Lebanon also involved Casey as he had already formed an alliance with Bashir Gemayel and the Phalangists, being instrumental in linking the warlord with the Mossad, thus making the Christian leader a shared asset. Even after the 1983 agreement between Lebanon and Israel, Amin Gemayel, who had become President following the assassination of his brother, allowed Lebanese intelligence to maintain contact with the Mossad over the disposition of the Palestinians. Woodward also considers the link between the CIA and the Mossad in the arms-for-hostages deal in 1984, Mossad's refusal to become involved in the US raids on Libya, and the Jonathan Jay Pollard spy trial in 1985. The work was based on interviews, official US documents, and news reports. It also has a chronology of covert operations in Central America and a glossary of acronyms.

211 Spy, steal and smuggle: Israel's special relationship with the United States.
Claudia Wright.   Belmont, Massachusetts: Association of Arab University Graduates, 1986. 32p.

An Arab-sponsored pamphlet which centres on Israeli intelligence activity within the United States through the Mossad. The prime objective of such activity is the acquisition of US defence technology.

Rescue Operations

212 **The smuggling of the Ethiopian Falasha to Israel through Sudan.**
Ahmed Karadawi. *African Affairs*, vol. 90, no. 358 (1991), p. 23-49. bibliog.
Karadawi discusses the details of the operation mounted to smuggle Ethiopian Jews from the Sudan to Israel between 1979 and 1985. The operation was mounted by the Mossad, the CIA, and the Sudanese State Security Service.

213 **Operation Thunder: the Entebbe raid: the Israeli's own story.**
Yehuda Ofer. London: Penguin, 1976. 141p.
Originally published in Hebrew as *Operation Jonathan: liberation from Entebbe* (Tel Aviv: Massada Press, 1976), this is an illustrated account of the rescue operation mounted by the Israelis to release the hostages at Entebbe airport in Uganda. Ofer covers the political background to the decision to mount the raid, negotiations between the Mossad and Kenyan intelligence services to enable the raid to take place, the raid itself, and the successful outcome.

214 **Operation Moses: the story of the exodus of the Falasha Jews from Ethiopia.**
Tudor Parfitt. London: Weidenfeld & Nicolson, 1985. 132p. bibliog.
An illustrated account of the rescue of the Falasha, the Ethiopian Jews, which largely took place in 1984 though there had been a trickle prior to that date. The work is largely based on interviews with members of international relief organizations, journalists, diplomats, and Sudanese and Israeli officials, following a commission from the Minority Rights Group to investigate the plight of the Falasha who had fled persecution and famine only to be further persecuted in the refugee camps. The author interviewed Mossad agents in the Sudan involved in the operation, but the names have been withheld because, at the time of publication, the operation was still in progress. The work traces the history of the Falasha Jews, the debate within Israel as to whether they should be regarded as Jews, and their loss from the Jewish world until the end of the eighteenth century. The pressure to rescue the Falasha gained force in Israel

Rescue Operations

through the work of a committee of Falasha who had managed to find refuge in Israel in the 1970s. The Israeli government decided in February 1980 to place the rescue in the hands of the Mossad who established a presence in the Sudan and worked with elements of the Sudanese Secret Service. Initially Kenya was used as a transit route with the co-operation of the Kenyan authorities and the CIA, though the operation was cloaked in secrecy. The situation was complicated by the unofficial actions of North American pro-Falasha groups who insisted on mounting amateur operations. The actions of these groups resulted in the closure of the Kenyan route in 1983, by which time 600 Falasha had been smuggled into Israel. The operation then switched to the Sudan and the Mossad provided funding to buy forged passports and block visas, and to bribe the Sudanese military to keep away from sensitive areas and turn a blind eye to Mossad activities in the Sudan. Although the Mossad operation was proceeding it was cloaked in secrecy for obvious reasons and the Israeli government came under criticism in the United States and at home. By 1984 the situation was critical, with a large number of Falasha dying in refugee camps, and it was decided to effect a massive airlift of the Ethiopian Jews from Sudan to Israel, though Operation Moses had to remain secret, as the Sudan could not be seen to be helping Jews. Unfortunately the secret airlift was exposed before all of the Falasha could be rescued and the exposure, which caused the operation to be terminated, was regarded with fury by the Falasha community in Israel. Further minor operations were mounted from the Sudan but the Mossad programme, although eminently successful, was prematurely terminated by the appearance in the Hebrew periodical *Nekuda* of hints of the operation, hints which were then repeated in the Israeli tabloid press. As with many other such operations the Israeli government and the Mossad had been forced to endure public criticism from within Israel and the wider Jewish community about apparent inactivity and indifference whilst, in reality, a major Mossad operation was under way.

215 Redemption song: the story of Operation Moses.
Louis Rapaport. London; New York: Harcourt, Brace, Jovanovich, 1986. 234p. bibliog.

This is an account of the airlift rescue of 8,000 Ethiopian Jews between November 1984 and March 1985. The Mossad played a major role in the organization of this rescue working in co-operation with the CIA and the Sudanese Secret Service.

216 Secret exodus.
Claire Safran. London; New York: Prentice Hall, 1987. 180p. bibliog.

An illustrated account of the series of semi-secret operations, including Operation Moses, which brought some 16,000 of the Falasha, the Black Jews of Ethiopia, to Israel between 1977 and 1985. This alone was a major operation, but the work also covers the role of the Mossad in moving other small groups to Israel by a variety of means. The work is based on interviews with the refugees themselves, United States officials, and operational Mossad agents. There are numerous references to the Israeli secret operations and the role of the Mossad.

Rescue Operations

217 **Operation 'Yakhin': the secret immigration of Moroccan Jews to Israel.**
Samuel Segev. Tel Aviv: Israeli Ministry of Defence, 1984.
(In Hebrew).

218 **Those who are called.**
Ian Traynor. *Guardian* (London), (10 Dec. 1994), p. 14-15, 18, 20, 23.

Traynor's article appeared in the Weekend section and reports on an operation mounted by the Mossad, with assistance from Zionists and Balkan warlords, to remove the Jews from Bosnia.

219 **Counterstrike Entebbe.**
Tony Williamson. London: Collins, 1976. 184p. maps.

Williamson's account of the Israeli raid on Entebbe is based on interviews with Israeli ministers, generals and senior officials, and on the testimonies of the hostages and the air crew. He also covers the discussions and debates that took place in Tel Aviv before the decision was taken to launch the attack, and of the intricate planning that went into every phase of the operation. The Mossad were heavily involved in the planning process and negotiations with the Kenyan authorities over support facilities for the operation.

Indexes

There follow three separate indexes: authors (personal and corporate); titles; and subjects. Title entries are italicized and refer either to the main titles, or to other works cited in the annotations. The numbers refer to bibliographical entry rather than page numbers. Individual index entries are arranged in alphabetical sequence.

Index of Authors

A

Aburish, Said K. 1
Adams, James 48, 159, 170
Allen, Thomas B. 2
Astor, Gerald 106

B

Badri, Hassan El 114
Bahbah, Bishara 160
Bar-Joseph, Uri 176
Bar-Zohar, Michel 49, 134
Bashkin, V. 31
Bauer, Yehuda 90
Becker, Jillian 135
Becket, Henry S. A. 3
Beit-Hallahmi, Benjamin 161
Ben-Ami, Yitshaq 91
Ben-Gurion, David 107
Bercuson, David J. 92
Beres, Louis Rene 50
Beyer, Lisa 136
Bhatia, Shyam 51
Bill, Jonas A. 187
Black, Ian 32
Blitzer, Wolf 188-9
Blum, Andrew 190
Blum, William 191
Blumberg, Stanley A. 33
Blundell, Nigel 4
Boar, Roger 4
Brenner, Lenni 34
Breslau, Karen 27
Brown, Derek 137
Buranelli, Nan 5
Buranelli, Vincent 5
Bushinsky, Jay 35

C

Carlson, John Roy 93
Carmel, Hesi 36
Cobban, Helena 138
Cockburn, Andrew 192
Cockburn, Leslie 192
Cooley, John K. 139, 162

D

Dag, Christopher 158
Dan, Ben 52
Dan, Uri 53, 57
Darvi, Andrea 44
Davenport, Elaine 54
Dayan, Moshe 115
Deacon, Richard [pseud.] 6-7, 55
Dekel, Efraim 94
Derogy, Jacques 36
Dobson, Christopher 8, 140

Doerner, William R. 164
Doran, Gideon 37-8
Dropkin, N. 165
Dupuy, T. N. 116

E

Eddy, Paul 54
Eisenberg, Dennis 57
Emerson, Steve 58, 193
Epstein, Edward J. 194
Esterow, Milton 59
Eytan, Steve 39

F

Field, Howard 60
Findley, Paul 195
Follath, Erich 61
Frankel, William 40
Friedman, Robert I. 196-7

G

Gabriel, Richard A. 141
Gertz, Bill 166
Gillman, Peter 54
Golan, Matti 10
Gosch, John 89
Green, Stephen 198

61

Gross, Ken 62-3
Groussard, Serge 142

H

Haber, Eitan 134
Hadari, Ze'ev Venia 95
Hagai, Eshed 64
Halevy, D. 148
Handel, Michael I. 117, 176
Harel, Isser 108
Harkabi, Yehashofat 118
Hart, Alan 143
Heikal, Mohamed 119
Henderson, Bernard R. 199
Hersh, Seymour M. 200
Hillal, Shlomo 171
Hirst, David 144
Hogg, Andrew 167
Horowitz, Dan 87
Hoy, Claire 65
Hunter, Jane 204

I

Iyad, Abu 146
Iyer, Pico 109

J

Jenish, D'Arcy 172
Jonas, George 67

K

Kam, Ephraim 120
Karadawi, Ahmed 212
Karpel, Craig S. 68, 178
Katz, Samuel M. 41, 85
Kelly, James 179
Khaled, Leila 147
Kimche, David 96
Kimche, Jon 96
Kurzman, Don 11

L

Landau, Eli 57
Lanir, Zvi 42

Laqueur, Walter 12-13, 121
Larkin, Margaret 122
Larteguy, Jean 86
Lawson, Mark 69
Levins, Hoag 123
Levite, Ariel 14
Lilienthal, Alfred M. 70
Livingstone, Neil C. 15, 148
Lotz, Wolfgang. 71
Lowther, William 173
Luttwak, Edward 87

M

McCormick, Donald see Deacon, Richard
McKinnon, Don 174
Maas, Peter 203
Magdoub, Taha El- 114
Malkin, Peter Z. 110
Manning, Paul 111
Ma'oz, Moshe Asad 16
Marshall, Jonathan 204
Masland, Tom 72
Melman, Yossi 46
Mercier, Jacques 73
Middleton, Drew 17
Moniteil, Vincent 74
Monroe, Elizabeth 124
Morgan-Wilts, Max 81, 169
Morris, Benny 32
Mozeson, Isaac 88

N

Nahas, Dunia 152
Nakdiman, Shlomo 175
Naylor, R. T. 43
Neff, Donald 125
Newman, Barbara 180
Nicosia, Francis R. 97
Nolkman, Ernest 18

O

O'Ballance, Edgar 126-7
Ofer, Dalia 98

Ofer, Yehuda 213
O'Neill, Bard E. 150
Ophir, Ephraim 99
Ostrovsky, Victor 65
Owens, Gwinn 33

P

Pakower, Mority Noam 100
Palmer, Norman 2
Parfitt, Tudor 214
Payne, Ronald 8, 75
Pearlman, Moshe 112
Pedatzur, Reuven 38
Perl, William R. 101
Perlmutter, Amos 89, 176
Perry, Victor 76
Persico, Joseph E. 205
Peters, Joan 128
Plate, Thomas 44
Posner, Gerald 113
Posner, Steve 45, 77

R

Rabinovich, Abraham 77
Randal, Jonathan 151, 181
Rapaport, Louis 215
Raviv, Dan 46
Rayyes, Riad El- 152
Richelson, Jeffrey T. 19
Ronnen, Meir 78
Roosevelt, Archibald Bulloch 20
Rose, David 153
Rosenthal, Monroe 88
Rothstein, Raphael 88, 155
Rouleau, Eric 146
Rubenstein, Richard E. 21
Rusbridger, James 22
Russell, George 154

S

Sachar, Howard M. 23
Safran, Claire 216
Salpeter, Eliahu 206
Satchell, Michael 207

Schack, Howard M. 79
Schiff, Ze'ev 102, 155, 182
Schofield, C. H. 183
Scott, Peter Dale 204
Seale, Patrick 156
Segev, Samuel 168, 217
Shiffer, Simon 184
Shlaim, Avraham 129
Smith, William E. 185, 208-9
Stein, Harry 110
Stein, Janice Gross 89, 130
Steven, Stewart 80
Stone, I. F. 103
Sumaida, Hussein 177
Sunday Times Insight Team 131
Sykes, Christopher 104

Szulc, Tad 105

T

Temko, N. 24
Teveth, Shabtai 25
Theodoulou, Mike 157
Thomas, Gordon 81, 169
Thompson, Leroy 26
Tinnin, David B. 158
Todd, David 82
Traynor, Ian 218

W

Waldrop, Theresa 27
Wall, James M. 83

Ware, John 113
Watson, Russell 84
West, Nigel 28
Williamson, Tony 219
Winston, Emanuel A. 29
Woodward, Bob 210
Wright, Claudia 211

Y

Ya'ari, Ehud 182
Yaniv, Avner 186

Z

Zohdy, Mohammed El din 114

Index of Titles

A

Abu Nidal: a gun for hire 156
Age of terrorism 12
Agronat Report: a partial report by the Commission of Inquiry 30
Alchemists of revolution: terrorism in the modern world 21
Alter ego on the loose 69
Anatomy of a covert operation: inside Israel's secret army 48
Arab-guerrilla power 1967-1972 126
Arab–Israeli war, October 1973: background and events 124
Arab reach: the secret war against Israel 123
Arafat: terrorist or peacemaker? 143
Arms and the man: Dr. Gerald Bull, Iraq and the supergun 173
As Israel tries to smother his book, a former Mossad spy spills some dark secrets of that shadowy service 63
Assassination of PLO man leaves trail of shadows 151
Assignment murder: how Israel planned the killing of Arafat's right-hand man 133
Averting Armageddon: the Pope, diplomacy and the pursuit of peace 81

B

Beirut spy 1
Ben-Gurion: prophet of fire 11
Ben-Gurion: the burning ground 1886-1948 25
Between Washington and Jerusalem 188
Black September: its short violent history 140
Blood libel: the inside story of General Ariel Sharon's history-making suit against Time magazine 53
Blood of Israel: the massacre of Israeli athletes in the 1972 Olympics 142
Boats of Cherbourg 77
Bullseye – one reactor 174
Bull's eye: the assassination and life of supergun inventor Gerald Bull 170
By way of deception: an insider's devastating exposé of the Mossad 58, 60, 63, 65-6, 72, 82

C

'C': a biography of Sir Maurice Oldfield, Head of MI6 6
Cairo to Damascus 93
Capture of Adolf Eichmann 112
Casey: the lives and secrets of William J. Casey: from the OSS to the CIA 205
Champagne Spy: Israel's master spy tells his story 71
C.I.A.: a forgotten history 191
Circle of fear 177
Counterstrike Entebbe 219
Covenant: love and death in Beirut 180
Crossroads of modern warfare: sixteen twentieth century battles 17
Crossroads to Israel: Palestine from Balfour to Bevin 104

D

Dangerous liaison: the inside story of the US–Israeli covert relationship 192
Deadly cycle of revenge 137
Death in Paris: mystery surrounds the assassination of a PLO leader on a secret mission 163
Deception: the invisible war between the KGB and the CIA 194
Decline of the superspies 56
Dictionary of espionage: spookspeak into English 3
Dilemmas of security: politics, strategy and the Israeli experience in Lebanon 186
Dirty business as usual for death or glory men 51
Dossier secret sur Israël: le terrorisme 74

E

Eagle and the lion: tragedy of American–Iranian relations 187
Eichmann in my hands 110
Eli Cohen: le combattant de Damas 73
Elusive security: the military and political geography of south Lebanon 183
Elusive victory: the Arab–Israeli wars 1947-1974 116
Every spy a prince: the complete history of Israel's intelligence 46
Ex-spy says U.S. indicted him for role in Pan-Am case 190

F

Failures in National Intelligence estimates: the case of the Yom Kippur war 129
Fedayeen: the story of the Palestinian guerrillas 155
First strike: the exclusive story of how Israel foiled Iraq's attempt to get the bomb 175
Flight and rescue 90
For lust of knowing: memoirs of an intelligence officer 20
Foreign intelligence organizations 19
Four-front war: from the Holocaust to the Promised Land 101
Freedom will be the death of him 153
From Tel Aviv: spies and spooks 35
From time immemorial: the origins of the Arab–Jewish conflict over Palestine 128
Fundamental surprise: the national intelligence crisis 42
Future of espionage 9

G

Gadaffi courts Israel in $1bn diplomacy drive 167
Games of intelligence: the classified conflict of international espionage 28
General loses his case 179
Greatest spies and spymasters 4
Green March, Black September 139
Guards without frontiers: Israel's war against terrorism 41
Guerrillas for Palestine 152
Gun and the olive branch: the roots of violence in the Middle East 144

H

Histoire secrète d'Israël 1917-1977 36
History of Israel: from the rise of Zionism to our time 23
History of the Israeli army (1974 to the present) 102
Hit team: the exciting story of Israel's strike against terrorists in Europe 158
Hot money and the politics of debt 43
House on Garabaldi Street 108
Hunting Black September: now it can be told 145

I

I can kill him now: inside Israel's decisions to hit – and not to hit Arafat 136
I regret nothing but the time for killing is over 157
Imperfect spies: the history of Israeli intelligence see *Every spy a prince*
Inside the Mossad: Israel tries to ban a book 72
Inside the PLO: covert units, secret funds and the war against Israel and the United States 148
Intelligence and strategic surprises 14
Intelligence game: illusions and delusion of international terrorism 22
Iran connection: secret teams and covert operations in the Reagan era 204
Iranian triangle: the untold story of Israel's role in the Iran–Contra affair 168
Iron Wall: Zionist revisionism from Jacotinsky to Shamir 34
Israel: a personal history 107
Israel blocks embarrassing book briefly in U.S., Canada 66
Israel: foreign intelligence and security services 201
Israel observed: an anatomy of the state 40
Israel: the man from the Mossad 78
Israel undercover: secret warfare and hidden diplomacy in the Middle East 45

Israeli army 87
Israeli connection: who Israel arms and why 161
Israeli intelligence over the years 76
Israeli intelligence: tactics, strategy and prediction 37
Israeli intelligence: utility and cost-effectiveness in policy formation 38
Israeli secret services 55
Israeli special services: instruments of aggression and terror 31
Israeli spies in the US 202
Israelis to advise Chamorro's spies 166
Israel's diplomatic offensive in Africa: the case of Zaïre 165
Israel's elite intelligence corps: exploits of the accomplished and respected 'Eye of David' 61
Israel's fateful decisions 118
Israel's Lebanon war 182
Israel's military relationship with Ecuador and Argentina 160
Israel's secret wars: the untold history of Israeli intelligence 32

J

Jay Pollard's peculiar tale 207
Jews were expendable: Free World diplomacy and the Holocaust 100

L

Land for peace? Shultz wings in as a familiar debate rages 164

Last Nazi: the life and times of Joseph Mengele 106
Libyan sandstorm 162
Long arm of the Mossad; a rabbi's son spills some Israeli nuclear secrets 84

M

Man of mystery sells a chilling story and then vanishes 62
Man with the golden gun 172
Manhunt: the incredible pursuit of a CIA agent turned terrorist 203
Martin Bormann: Nazi in exile 111
Master of mystery and murder; for the shadowy Abu Nidal, terror is a way of life 154
Mengele mystery; as new revelations multiply, the question remains: is this the Nazi doctor? 109
Mengele: the complete story 113
Merchants of treason: America's secrets for sale 2
Message from Mossad 149
Military deception, strategic surprise and conventional deterrence 89
Mossad: Israel's most secret service 75
Mossad: Israel's secret intelligence service 75
Mossad linked to WTC bomb suspect 196
Mossad's might: an Israeli agent comes in from the cold 82
My home, my land: a narrative of the Palestinian struggle 146

My people shall live: an autobiography of a revolutionary 147

N

1973 intelligence failure: a reconsideration 130
No victors, no vanquished: the Yom Kippur war 127
Nuclear arms and the missing man 83

O

L'Oeil de Tel-Aviv 39
On the second immigration from Romania and its way 99
One man Mossad: Reuven Shiloah father of Israeli intelligence 64
Onward Christian diplomats 178
Operation Babylon: the story of the rescue of the Jews of Iraq 171
Operation Jonathan: liberation from Entebbe 213
Operation Moses: the story of the exodus of the Falasha Jews from Ethiopia 214
Operation Peace for Galilee: the Israeli–PLO war in Lebanon 141
Operation Shylock 69
Operation Thunder: the Entebbe raid: the Israeli's own story 213
Operation 'Yakhin': the secret immigration of Moroccan Jews to Israel 217

P

Painter, poet, soldier, spy 59

Palestine Liberation Organization: people, power and politics 138
PLO: the rise and fall of the Palestine Liberation Organization 135
Plumbatt affair 54
Pollard: the spy's legacy 199
Pontiff: inside the Vatican – behind today's sensational headlines 169
Price of power: Kissinger in the Nixon White House 200

Q

Quest for the Red Prince 134

R

Ramadan war, 1973 114
Redemption song: the story of Operation Moses 215
Rescue of European Jewry and illegal immigration to Palestine 98
Rescuers: the world top anti-terrorist units 26
Revolutionary warfare in the Middle East: the Israelis vs the Fedayeen 150
Road to peace: a biography of Shimon Peres 10
Road to Ramadan 119
Road to war 1967: the origins of the Arab–Israeli conflict 121

S

Second exodus 95

Secret alliance: the extraordinary story of the rescue of Jews 105
Secret army 92
Secret exodus 216
Secret police: the inside story of a network of terror 44
Secret roads: the illegal migration of a people 96
Secret warriors: inside the covert military operations of the Reagan era 193
Secrets of a spymaster: East Germany's top spook talks about his craft 27
Security or Armageddon: Israel's nuclear strategy 50
Shai: the exploits of Hagana intelligence 94
Six days of Yad-Mordechai 122
Smuggling of the Ethiopian Falasha to Israel through Sudan 212
Snowball: the story behind the Lebanon war 184
Soldier spies: Israeli military intelligence 85
Sphynx of Damascus: a political biography 16
Spies in the Promised Land: Isar Harel and the Israeli Secret Service 49
Spook Kook 58
Spyclopaedia: the comprehensive handbook of espionage 7
Spy/counterspy: an encyclopaedia of espionage 5
Spy from Israel 52
Spy in Canaan: my life as a Jewish-American businessman spying for Israel in Arab lands 79

Spy, steal and smuggle: Israel's special relationship with the United States 211
Spying between friends: the Pollard verdict causes a wave of unease in Israel 208
Spymasters of Israel 80
Story of my life 115
Surprise attack: the victim's perspective 120
Survival factor: Israeli intelligence from World War I to the present 33

T

Taking sides: America's secret relations with a militant Israel 198
Tales of the Mossad 68
Temporary ban on Mossad book is overturned in U.S. and Canada 60
Territory of lies: the exclusive story of Jonathan Jay Pollard 189
They dare to speak out 195
Third Reich and the Palestine question 97
Those who are called 218
To win or die: a personal narrative of Menachen Begin 24
Tragedy of Lebanon: Christian warlords, Israeli adventurers and American bunglers 181
Triple trouble in Israel 206
Two minutes over Baghdad 176

U

Underground to Palestine and reflections thirty years later 103

Unnatural alliance 159
Unorthodox Rabbi 197
Untold history of Israel 36
Uproar over a spy: the Pollard case sparks new US–Israeli tensions 209
U.S. Intelligence Agencies and activities: the performance of the intelligence community 132

V

Veil: the secret wars of the CIA 1981-1987 210
Vengeance: the true story of a counter-terrorism mission 67
Verdict is guilty 185
Vital intelligence: a nation's right 29

W

Walls of Israel 86
War against terror: national policy and security of Israel 1975-88 47
War against terrorism 15
War, strategy and intelligence 117
War without end; the terrorists: an intelligence dossier 8
Warriors for Jerusalem: the six days that changed the Middle East 125
Warriors of the night: spies, soldiers and American intelligence 18
Wars of the Jews: a military history from Biblical to modern times 88
World of secrets: the uses and limits of intelligence 23

Y

Years of wrath, days of glory 91
Yom Kippur war 131

Z

Zionist connection: what price peace? 70

Index of Subjects

A

Aaronsohn family
  membership of NILI 88
Abu Iyad
  biography of 146
  Mossad operations against 32, 41
  role in Al Fatah 146
Abu Jihad
  assassination of 133
  Mossad operations against 41, 149, 180
Abu Nidal 16
  activities of 12, 154
  assassination of Atef Bseiso 163
  biography of 156
  inter-factional activities 156
  leadership of Al Fatah 154
  Mossad operations against 148, 154, 156
Adwan, Kamal
  assassination of 70
Africa
  Mossad training role 161
Agranot Commission of Inquiry
  recommendations of 38, 130
  Report 30
Ajaz, Ahmed
  involvement in World Trade Centre bombing 196
  Mossad mole? 196
Al Fatah *see* Fatah, Al
Aman
  Commission of Inquiry into 30, 38
  Egyptian intelligence failures 75
  relations with Mossad 80, 85, 87
  role in Six Day war 121
  role in Yom Kippur war 14, 19, 23, 30, 89, 114, 116, 119-20, 124, 130-2
  role of 32, 38, 85
American-Jewish community: adverse reaction to Pollard affair 209
American Jewish Joint Distribution Committee
  role in illegal immigration 105
American Jews
  support for illegal immigration 105
Amit, Meir
  directorship of Mossad 46
Arab front-line states
  role in terrorism 15
Arab guerrilla power
  growth of 126
Arab guerrilla warfare 93
Arab–Israeli conflict
  origins 128, 144
Arab–Israeli wars 115-16, 121
  role of Mossad 31, 36, 46, 115, 117
Arab States
  impact of Israeli Intelligence Services 35
  support for Palestinian guerrillas 123
Arafat, Yasser 24, 168
  biography of 143
  Israeli actions against 136
  peace negotiations with Israel 157
  relations with Al Fatah 143
  relations with Black September 143
Argentina
  Israeli military connections 160
Asad, President
  biography of 16
Avigir, Shaul
  role in Mossad 90, 105
Aviv, Juval
  former Mossad operative 190
  prosecution for US mail fraud 190
  report on Pan-Am bombing 190

B

Baader-Meinhof
  links with Black September 140
Balkans
  use as transit centre for illegal immigration 95
Begin, Menachen
  biography of 24
  leadership of Jewish underground 24
  premiership of 118
Beirut
  bombing of marine barracks intelligence 58, 63
  St George Hotel use by agents 1
Ben-Gurion
  biography of 11, 25
  leadership of Jewish underground 25
Bennett, Max
  arrest of 75

71

Black September
  activities of 15, 140
  assassination of Baruch
    Cohen 136, 146
  hijack operations 140
  letter bomb campaign
    140, 200
  links with
    Baader-Meinhof 140
  links with Japanese Red
    Army 140
  Mossad operations
    against 20, 41,
    139-40, 142, 144-6,
    152, 200
  Munich Olympic Games
    massacre 67, 136,
    139-40, 142, 145-6,
    155, 200
  origins of 152
  relations with Yasser
    Arafat 143
  structure of 140
Bormann, Martin
  Mossad hunt for 111
Bosnia
  rescue of Jews by
    Mossad 218
Brichah
  role in illegal
    immigration 90
Bseiso, Atef
  assassination of 151,
    163
Bull, Gerald
  arms trade with South
    Africa 172
  assassination of 170
  murder by Mossad
    charge 32, 170, 172-3
  role in Iraq supergun
    affair 170, 172-3

C

Cairo Radio
  anti-Israeli propaganda
    125
Casey, William J.
  biography of 205, 210
  directorship of CIA 205,
    210

Central Intelligence
    Agency (CIA)
  activities of 28
  directorship of William
    J. Casey 205, 210
  Middle East operations
    194
  relations with Mossad
    13, 56, 61, 188, 191,
    194, 202, 210, 214-16
  relations with Shin Bet
    56
  report on Israeli
    Intelligence Services
    201
  role in Ethiopian Jews
    rescue 212
  role in Middle East 125
Champagne Spy see Lotz,
    Wolfgang
Cherbourg patrol boats
  seizure by Mossad 39,
    55, 77
Cohen, Baruch
  assassination by Black
    September 136, 146
Cohen, Eli
  biography of 52, 73
  impact on Six Day war
    52
  operations in Syria 4,
    52, 55, 73, 85-6
counter-terrorism 12
  account of 15
  Israeli agencies 15
counter-terrorism force
  survey of 26
Cyprus
  assassination of Al
    Fatah agents 164
  bombing of Palestinian
    car ferry 164

D

Davison, Ian
  assassination of Mossad
    agents 157
Dayan, Moshe
  biography of 115
DGSE
  activities of 28

Dimna nuclear research
    station
  weapons stockpile
    revealed 48, 56, 62,
    83-4

E

East Germany
  operations against
    Mossad 27
Ecuador
  Israeli military
    connections 160
Egypt
  activities of Wolfgang
    Lotz 4, 55, 61, 71
  Aman intelligence
    failures 75
  attack on Yad-
    Mordechai 122
  Lavon affair 87
  Mossad intelligence
    failures 75
  Mossad operation
    against rocket
    programme 46, 49,
    71, 85
  radar system captured
    by Mossad 39
  rescue of Jewish
    population 32
Eichmann, Adolf
  kidnapping of 39, 55-7,
    59, 61, 75, 77-8, 80,
    107-8, 110, 112
  role of Peter Malkin 59,
    78
  trial of 4
Entebbe operation
  intelligence role of
    Howard Schack
    79
  political background
    213
  role of Mossad 10, 32,
    46, 55, 213, 219
  use of Kenya as transit
    base 10, 213-14
espionage
  encyclopaedia of 5, 7
  glossary of terms 2-3

Ethiopia
  rescue of Jewish
    population 32, 106,
    212, 214-16
  role of CIA in rescue of
    Jewish population
    212

F

Falasha
  history of 214
  rescue from Ethiopia
    32, 106, 212, 214-16
Far East
  Mossad training role
    161
Fatah, Al 16, 141
  activities of 12, 15, 154
  assassination of agents
    by Mossad 164
  leadership of Abu Nidal
    154
  origins of 152
  relations with Yasser
    Arafat 143
  role of 138
  role of Abu Iyad 146
Fedayeen
  expulsion from Jordan
    126, 147
  Lod airport massacre
    155
  origins of 155
foreign volunteers
  role in 1948 war 92
France
  patrol boat sale to Israel
    blocked 39, 55, 77
  relations with 46
French intelligence
  complicity in Atef
    Bseiso assassination
    163

G

Gadaffi, Colonel
  attempts to improve
    relations with USA
    167

Gemayel, Bashir
  biography of 180
  Mossad relations with
    46, 53, 179, 182, 210
Gestapo
  co-operation with
    Mossad Aliyah Bet
    97
Great Britain
  arrest of Ismael Sowan
    153
  Mossad covert
    operations 153
Greenwald, Ronald
  branded as Mossad
    agent 197
GRU
  activities of 28

H

Habash, George 141
  activities of 12, 15
Haganah
  activities of 34, 94
  establishment of 55, 93
  membership of Isser
    Harel 49
  membership of
    Wolfgang Lotz 71
  role in illegal
    immigration 55
  role of 33
Harel, Isser
  biography of 49
  directorship of Mossad
    46, 49, 55, 57, 75
  directorship of Shin Bet
    46
  Intelligence Agencies
    directorship 85
  membership of Haganah
    49
Hebrew Immigrant Aid
  Society
  role in illegal
    immigration 105
Hertzog, Chaim
  role in intelligence 75
Heydrick, Richard
  role in Jewish illegal
    immigration 97

I

illegal immigration 139
  American Jewish
    support 105
  organization of 11
  role of Berthold
    Stomfer 98
  role of Brichah 90
  role of Haganah 55
  role of Hebrew
    Immigrant Aid
    Society 105
  role of Jewish Agency
    for Palestine 94-5
  role of Mossad Aliyah
    Bet 32-3, 46, 55, 75,
    90-1, 94-9, 104-5, 144
  role of Nazi authorities
    97
  role of Romanian
    government 99
  use of Balkans as transit
    centre 95
  use of Yugoslavia as
    transit centre 90
intelligence gathering 12
international
  money-lending
  role of intelligence
    services 43
international terrorism
  account of 15
  chronology of 8
Iran
  clandestine relations
    with Israel 168
  Mossad operations 51
  relations with Israel 12
  relations with United
    States 187
Iran–Contra affair 187,
  204
  role of Israel 168, 206
  role of Mossad 168,
    204-5
Iraq
  Mossad capture of
    MiG21 fighter 32, 39,
    55, 87
  Israeli Air Force raid on
    nuclear reactor 24,
    61-2

Iraq *contd.*
  Mossad operations 24,
    39, 51, 177, 210
  rescue of Jewish
    population 106, 171
  supergun affair 170,
    172-3
Iraqi nuclear programme
  Mossad operations 79
Iraqi nuclear reactor
  Israeli raid on 24,
    174-6
  role of Mossad 50, 61,
    174-6, 210
Irgun
  establishment of 55
  operations 91
Islamic Jihad 137
  activities of 21
Israel
  actions against Yasser
    Arafat 136
  armed forces 40
  arms deals with
    Argentina 160
  arms deals with South
    Africa 206
  attempt to ban
    Ostrovsky book 63,
    66, 72, 82
  clandestine relations
    with Iran 168
  electoral system 40
  history of 23
  intelligence agencies
    19, 20
  intelligence strategy 37
  Knesset 40
  legal system 40
  media 40
  nuclear programme 50
  nuclear stockpile
    revealed 48, 56, 62,
    83-4
  Palestinian policies 118
  peace negotiations with
    Palestinians 157
  political parties 40
  raid on Iraqi nuclear
    reactor 24, 61-2
  reaction to Pollard affair
    208
  relations with France 46

relations with Iran 12,
  168
relations with South
  Africa 159
religious establishment
  40
restoration of
  diplomatic relations
  with Zaïre 165
role in terrorism 74
role of foreign
  volunteers 92
security policies 47
United States lobbying
  195
uranium ore seizure 54
Israeli Defence Forces
  86-7
  role in assassination of
    Abu Jihad 133
  role of 41, 47
  special units 26
  survey of 102
Israeli Intelligence
  Services 42
  accountability of 38
  activities 32, 34, 39
  anti-Arab activities 33,
    35
  CIA report on 201
  role of 29, 38, 46

J

Japanese Red Army
  links with Black
    September 140
Jewish Agency for
  Palestine
  role in illegal
    immigration 94-5
Jewish culture
  militancy in 88
Jewish illegal immigration
  European exodus 32
  role of Mossad Aliyah
    Bet 32
Jewish underground
  leadership of David
    Ben-Gurion 25
  leadership of Menachen
    Begin 24

Jibril, Ahmed
  Mossad operations
    against 41
Jordan
  expulsion of Palestinian
    guerrillas 126, 147

K

Kenya
  role in Entebbe
    operation 10, 213,
    219
  use as transit centre for
    Ethiopian Jews 10,
    213-14
Kenyan intelligence
  relations with Mossad
    10, 213
KGB
  activities of 28
  Middle East operations
    194
Khaled, Leila
  autobiography of 147
  operations with PFLP
    147
Khashoggi, Adnan
  role in Libyan attempt
    to improve US
    relations 167
Kimche, David
  career of 75
  intermediary in US–Iran
    arms negotiations
    206, 209
Kirkland, Brad
  role as Mossad double
    agent 45
Knesset
  workings of 40

L

Latin America
  Mossad training role
    161
Lebanese Christian
  Agency
  Jerusalem Office 178
  Mossad protection 178

Lebanese invasion,1982
  role of Mossad 45-6, 76,
    118, 135, 141, 181-4,
    186, 210
Lebanese Phalangists 141
  Palestinian refugee
    massacres 185
  relations with Mossad
    46, 179-81, 185, 210
Lebanon
  Israeli occupation of
    southern area 178
  Likud objectives 182
  Mossad assassination
    raids 70
  power struggle with
    Syria 178
  role of Mossad 75,
    178-86
Lechi
  establishment of 55
Libya
  intelligence activities
    19
  Mossad operations
    against 162, 169, 203
  terrorism activities 12,
    15
  US raids on 210
Likud
  Lebanese objectives
    182
  organization of 118
Lillehammer operation
  failure of 55, 70
Lod airport massacre
  role of Palestinian
    guerrillas 155
Lotz, Wolfgang
  activities of 4, 55, 61,
    75
  arrest of 71
  disclosure of Egyptian
    rocket programme 71
  membership of Haganah
    71
  release of 71

M

Mackenzie, Howard *see*
  Schack, Howard H.

Malkin, Peter
  biography of 59
  drawings of 78
  role in Eichmann
    operations 59, 78
Mbotu, President
  restoration of
    diplomatic relations
    with Israel 165
media
  role in counter-terrorism
    12
Mengele, Joseph
  biography of 106, 113
  death of 108
  Mossad hunt for 106,
    108, 113
MI5
  activities of 22, 28
  impact on Western
    culture 9
  tradecraft 3
MI6
  activities of 22, 28
  relations with Mossad 6
  tradecraft 3
Middle East
  international terrorism 8
Military Intelligence
  Commission of Inquiry
    into 30
  rivalry with 80
  role in Six Day war 121
  role in Yom Kippur war
    14, 19, 23, 30, 89,
    114, 116, 119-20,
    124, 130-2
  role of 38, 55
Morocco
  rescue of Jewish
    population 32, 46, 76,
    106, 217
Mossad
  Abu Iyad operations 32,
    41
  Abu Jihad operations
    41, 149, 180
  Abu Nidal operations
    148, 154, 156
  activities of 7, 17, 22,
    28, 31, 35-6, 39, 46,
    48, 51, 61, 65, 68,
    85-6

acquisition of Mirage
  fighter plans 55
Amit directorship 46
assassination of Abu
  Jihad 133
assassination of Al
  Fatah agents in
  Cyprus 264
assassination raids on
  Lebanon 70
assessment of Arab
  nuclear capability 50
attack by Ostrovsky 65
attempt to ban
  Ostrovsky book 63,
  66, 72, 82
Beirut bombing of
  marine barracks
  intelligence 58, 63
bombing of Palestinian
  car ferry in Cyprus
  164
Bull, Gerald
  assassination charge
  32
capture of MiG21
  aircraft 32, 39, 55, 87
career of David Kimche
  75
Cherbourg patrol boat
  seizure 39, 55, 77
CIA report on 201
circumvention of Arab
  economic boycott 123
Commission of Inquiry
  into 30, 38
counter-espionage role
  57, 75, 80, 126
counter-terrorism role 8,
  41, 140-1, 152
counter-terrorism
  operations 20, 45, 134
court action on
  Ostrovsky book 60
covert operations 187,
  204
covert operations in
  Great Britain 153
criticism of 46, 56, 65
description of 5
development of 92, 105
East German operations
  27

75

Mossad *contd.*
   effectiveness of 22, 28, 210
   efficiency of 75
   Egyptian intelligence failures 75
   Egyptian radar system captured 39
   Egyptian rocket operation 46, 49, 85
   Eichmann kidnapping 39, 55-7, 59, 61, 77-8, 80, 107-8, 110, 112
   Eli Cohen operations 4, 52, 55, 73, 85-6
   Entebbe operation 10, 32, 46, 55, 79, 213, 219
   establishment of 39, 46, 55, 57, 75, 80
   European operations 74, 105
   Far East training role 161
   foreign counter-intelligence training 34, 192
   foreign internal security forces training 34, 161, 165-6, 206
   founding members 97
   funding of 96
   Harel directorship 46, 49
   history of 46, 86
   hunt for Martin Bormann 111
   hunt for Mengele 106, 109, 113
   impact on Western culture 9
   implication in Bseiso assassination 151, 163
   implication in Fathi Shqaqi assassination 137
   implication in Gerald Bull murder 32, 170, 172-3
   infrastructure 32, 55, 96
   intelligence exchange with South Africa 159
   intelligence-gathering activities 16, 40-1, 45, 118, 187
   Iranian operations 51
   Iraqi nuclear reactor raid 24, 32, 39, 50-1, 79, 174-6, 210
   Iraqi operations 32, 51, 177
   Islamic Jihad operations 21
   Lebanese operations 75
   Libyan operations 162, 169, 203
   Lillehammer failure 55, 70
   modernization of 46
   money-laundering operations 43
   Mordechai Vananu kidnapping 48, 56, 62, 83-4, 209
   Moroccan Jews rescue 32, 46, 76, 106
   Munich Olympic Games operation 15, 45, 67, 134-6, 139-40, 142, 144-6, 200
   nuclear intelligence gathering 50, 123
   operation against Salameh 134
   Operation Suzanna 75-6
   operation to rescue Falasha 32
   operations against Ahmed Jibril 41
   operations against Black September 20, 41, 139-40, 142, 144-6, 152, 200
   operations against PFLP 20
   operations against PLO 41, 118, 148
   operations against US critics 195
   operations in Africa 34, 159, 161, 165, 206
   operations in the United States 2, 29, 206-8, 210-11
   operations on behalf of United States 192
   origins of 11, 25, 41, 96, 100-1, 103
   Palestinian guerrilla operations 45, 75-6, 126, 138, 143, 150-1
   Palestinian operations 31, 45, 51, 158
   Philip Roth as agent? 69
   Plumbatt operation 54, 61
   Pollard case 29, 32, 76, 168, 189, 199, 206-10
   recruitment of Wolfgang Lotz 71
   recruitment policy 61, 96
   refusal to join US Libyan raids 210
   relations with Aman 80, 85, 87
   relations with Bashir Gemayel 46, 53, 182, 210
   relations with CIA 13, 56, 61, 188, 191, 194, 202, 210, 212, 214-16
   relations with Kenyan intelligence 10, 213, 219
   relations with Lebanese Phalangists 46, 179-81, 185, 210
   relations with MI6 6
   relations with President Amin Gemayel 210
   relations with SAVAK 61
   relations with Sudanese State security 212, 214-16
   relations with United States intelligence 18, 35, 193, 198
   relations with Vatican 81
   rescue of Bosnian Jews 218
   rescue of Ethiopian Jews 32, 106, 212, 214-16

Mossad *contd.*
  rescue of Iraqi Jews
    106, 171
  rescue of Romanian
    Jews 106
  rescue of Syrian Jews 106
  rescue of Tunisian Jews
    32
  role in Arab–Israeli
    wars 31, 36, 46, 115,
    117
  role in Edwin P. Wilson
    arrest 203
  role in illegal
    immigration 75
  role in Iran–Contra
    affair 168, 204-5
  role in Lebanese
    invasion,1982 45-6,
    76, 118, 135, 141,
    181-4, 186, 210
  role in Middle East 6
  role in Six Day war 52,
    55, 57, 75, 121, 124-6
  role in US–Iran arms
    affair 209
  role in Yom Kippur war
    11, 14, 19, 23-4, 30,
    32, 35, 38, 55, 75, 89,
    114, 116, 119-20,
    124, 127, 129-32
  role of 32, 44, 102
  role of Reuven Shiloah
    64
  role of Shaul Avigir 90,
    105
  South African
    operations 34, 159-60,
    205
  South American
    operations 160, 192
  strategy of 37
  struggle against arms
    embargo 57
  survey of 26
  Syrian operations 4, 16,
    73, 169
  tradecraft 3, 110
  training policy 61, 161
  uranium acquisition
    operation 7
  use of PLO officials as
    agents 51

Mossad agents
  assassination of 136,
    146, 157
Mossad Aliyah Bet
  co-operation with
    Gestapo 97
  co-operation with
    Sicherheitsdienst 97
  formation of 32, 105
  role in illegal
    immigration 32-3, 46,
    55, 75, 90-1, 94-9,
    104-5, 144
  role of Shaul Avigir
    105
Munich Olympic Games
  massacre 12, 15, 45
  Mossad operation 67,
    134-6, 139, 142,
    144-6, 200
  role of Black September
    67, 136, 139-40, 142,
    144-6, 152, 155,
    200
Mussadiq
  overthrow of 187

N

Najjar, Mohammed
  Yusuf
  assassination of 70
Nanna, Sabri
  possible implication in
    Bseiso assassination
    151
Nasser, Kamal
  assassination of 70
National Police Border
  Guards
  role of 41
Nicaragua
  use of Mossad for
    security training 166
NILI network
  espionage operations
    128
  role of 33, 88
Nimrodi, Yaacov
  role in Libyan attempt
    to improve US
    relations 167

O

Operation Moses 212,
  214-16
Operation Suzanna 75-6
Operation Yakhim 217
Operation Shylock
  novel by Roth 69
Ossirah nuclear reactor
  intelligence role of
    Howard Schack 79
  Israeli raid on 24, 50,
    174-6
  role of Mossad 32, 50,
    61, 174-6, 210
Ostrovsky, Victor
  attack on Mossad 65
  attempted ban on book
    63, 66, 72, 82
  Beirut bombing
    accusation 58
  court action over book
    60
  criticism of 58
  interview with 63
  publication of
    biography 65, 82
  role as Mossad agent 63

P

Palamach
  establishment of 93
Palestine
  Israeli policies 118
Palestine Liberation
  Organization 16, 24,
    141, 168, 200
  activities of 12, 15, 17,
    21, 148
  aims 135
  assassination of Mossad
    agents 157
  covert units 148
  finances of 148
  infiltration by Mossad
    51
  infrastructure 148
  intelligence activities 19
  Mossad operations
    against 118
  political analysis of 138

77

Palestine Liberation
  Organization *contd.*
  structure 135
  tactics 135
Palestinian guerrillas
  assassination operations
    126
  expulsion from Jordan
    126, 147
  hijack operations 126,
    140
  letter bomb campaign
    158
  links with international
    terrorism 139
  Mossad operations
    against 45, 75-6, 138,
    143, 150-1
  rise of 139
  Shin Bet operations
    126, 150
  support by Arab States
    123
  terrorist operations 152,
    155
Palestinian refugees
  massacres by Lebanese
    Phalangists 185
Palestinian terrorist groups
  8, 134
Palestinians
  Mossad operations
    against 31, 158
Pan-Am bombing
  terrorist intelligence 190
Peres, Shimon
  biography of 10
PFLP
  hijacking operations 147
  membership of Leila
    Khaled 147
  Mossad operations 20
  origins of 20, 152
  terrorist campaign 20
Phalange movement 46,
  141, 179-81, 185
Plumbatt operation 54, 61
political terror
  account of 12
Pollard, Jonathan Jay
  espionage for Israel 29,
    32, 76, 168, 189, 199,
    206-10

Pollard affair
  effects on American
    Jewish community
    209
  effects on US–Israeli
    relations 208
Popular Front for the
  Liberation of
  Palestine *see* PFLP

R

Ragin, Yehuda
  founding member of
    Mossad 97
Ramadan war *see* Yom
  Kippur war
Red Prince *see* Salameh,
  Ali Hassan
Romania
  rescue of Jewish
    population 106
Romanian government
  role in illegal
    immigration 99
Roosevelt, Archibald
  Bulloch
  biography of 20
Roth, Philip
  agent for Mossad? 69
  Operation Shylock
    novel 69

S

St George Hotel, Beirut
  use by agents 1
Sabra refugee camp
  Israeli commission of
    inquiry 185
  massacre in 179, 182,
    185
Salameh, Ali Hassan
  control of Munich
    Olympic Games
    massacre 134
  Mossad operations
    against 134
SAVAK
  relations with Mossad
    61

Schack, Howard H.
  Entebbe operation
    intelligence 79
  Ossirah nuclear plant
    intelligence 79
  role as Mossad agent 79
Shah of Iran
  overthrow of 187
Shai
  establishment of 55
  operations of 94
Shamir, Yitzhat
  role in intelligence 75
Sharon, Ariel
  Time magazine libel
    action 53, 179
Shatilla refugee camp
  Israeli commission of
    inquiry 185
  massacre in 179, 182, 185
Shi'ite terrorist groups 8
Shiloah, Reuven
  role in Mossad 64
Shin Bet
  complicity in Arab
    hijackers murder 56
  counter-terrorism
    activities 152
  criticism of 56
  directorship of Isser
    Harel 46
  operations against
    Palestinian guerrillas
    126, 150
  relations with CIA 56
  role of 32, 41
  tarnished reputation of
    209
Shind, Ze'ev
  founding member of
    Mossad 97
Shqaqi, Fathi
  assassination of 137
Sicherheitsdienst
  co-operation with
    Mossad Aliyah Bet 97
Six Day war
  impact of Eli Cohen
    espionage 52
  role of military
    intelligence 121
  role of Mossad 52, 55,
    57, 75, 121, 124-6

South Africa
  arms deals with Gerald
    Bull 172
  arms deals with Israel
    206
  intelligence exchanges
    with Israel 159
  relations with Israel
    159
  use of Mossad for
    training 34, 159, 161,
    206
South America
  use of Mossad for
    counter-intelligence
    training 193
Sowan, Ismael
  arrest as Mossad agent
    153
Soviet Union
  espionage in the United
    States 2
Stasi
  impact on Western
    culture 9
Stern Gang 141
  activities of 34, 143
Stomfer, Berthold
  role in illegal
    immigration 98
Sudanese State Security
  relations with Mossad
    212, 214-16
  role in Ethiopian Jew
    rescue 212, 216
Sumeida, Hussein
  role in Iraqi intelligence
    177
  role as Mossad double
    agent 177
supergun affair 170, 177
  involvement of British
    companies 172
  murder of Gerald Bull
    170, 172-3
  role of Mossad 172
Syria
  Eli Cohen's espionage
    4, 52, 55, 73, 85-6
  guerrilla policy 125
  intelligence activities 19
  Mossad operations 4,
    16, 73, 169

power struggle in
    Lebanon 178
  rescue of Jewish
    population 106

T

terror
  sociology of 12
terrorism
  role of Arab front-line
    states 15
  relationship to social
    revolutions 21
terrorist organizations
  description of 8, 26
Topol, Haim
  former Mossad agent
    160
Tunisia
  rescue of Jewish
    population 32

U

United States
  foreign espionage
    successes 2
  impact of Pollard case
    189
  intelligence activities
    13
  lobbying by Israel 195
  Middle East policy
    misinterpretations 20
  Mossad operations in 2,
    29, 206-8, 210-11
  raids on Libya 210
  relations with Iran 187
  Soviet Union espionage
    2
  use of Mossad 192
United States
  counter-intelligence
    failure of 2
United States espionage
  cases
  chronology of 2
United States government
  infiltration by Zionists
    70

United States hostages
  Iran rescue attempt
    187
United States
  Intelligence
  failures of 18
  relations with Mossad
    18, 35, 193, 198
US–Iran arms affair
  role of Mossad 206, 209
United States Marine
  barracks, Beirut
  bombing of 63

V

Vananu, Mordechai
  kidnapping of 62, 83-4,
    209
  leaking of Israeli
    nuclear secrets 48, 56,
    62, 83-4
  trial of 48
Vatican
  relations with Mossad
    81

W

Wazir, Khalil al- see Abu
  Jihad
Western culture
  impact of espionage 9
Wilson, Edwin P.
  arrest of 203
  Libyan operations 203
Wolf, Marcus
  career of 27
Workers of Zion party
  origins 55
World Trade Centre
  bombing 196

Y

Yad-Mordechai
  Egyptian attack on 122
Yariv, Aharon
  security adviser to
    Golda Meir 145

Yassin, Adnan
  arrest by PLO as
    Mossad spy 51
Yehieli, Zvi
  founding member of
    Mossad 97
Yom Kippur war
  Arab misinformation
    campaign 24, 114,
    125
  intelligence analysis
    14
  intelligence failures
    132
  role of Military
    Intelligence 14, 19,
    23, 30, 89, 114, 116,
    119-20, 124, 130-2
  role of Mossad 11, 14,
    19, 23-4, 30, 32, 35,
    38, 55, 75, 89, 114,
    116, 119-20, 124,
    127, 129-32
  significance of 17
Yugoslavia
  use as transit centre for
    illegal immigration 90

Z

Zaïre
  provision of military
    training by Israel 165
  security forces training
    by Mossad 165

For Product Safety Concerns and Information please contact our EU
representative GPSR@taylorandfrancis.com
Taylor & Francis Verlag GmbH, Kaufingerstraße 24, 80331 München, Germany

www.ingramcontent.com/pod-product-compliance
Lightning Source LLC
Chambersburg PA
CBHW021146230426
43667CB00005B/271